Troubled Transplants

National Child Welfare Resource Center for Management and Administration

Troubled Transplants

Unconventional Strategies for Helping Disturbed Foster and Adoptive Children

*****

Richard J. Delaney, Ph.D.

Frank R. Kunstal, Ed.D.

National Child Welfare Resource Center for Management and Administration
Edmund S. Muskie Institute of Public Affairs
University of Southern Maine

1993

Delaney, Richard J.
Kunstal, Frank R.
Troubled Transplants: Unconventional Strategies for Helping Disturbed Foster
and Adoptive Children

Library of Congress Catalog Card Number: 92-61984
ISBN: 0-939561-14-X

Note to the Reader: The ideas, procedures, suggestions and strategies described
in this book are no substitute for collaboration by foster and adoptive parents
with helping professionals in their efforts to help disturbed children.

5th Printing

Printed in the United States of America

University of Southern Maine

Preface

Over the past thirty years, volumes have been written about the abused, neglected and sexually exploited child. Although some studies have touted the resiliency of maltreated children in their ability to rebound—relatively unscathed—from earlier maltreatment, more research has documented the lasting psychological injuries these unfortunate children have suffered. Sweeping societal problems with poverty, homelessness, drug and alcohol abuse, broken homes and "children-raising-children" have culminated in a staggering increase in child maltreatment. Currently, a rising tide of foster and adoptive children are flooding the welfare system. Many of these children exhibit severe difficulties in relating to others and in coping within family settings. (Indeed, a goodly number of these youngsters would have been, in years past, placed in residential child care facilities, psychiatric hospitals or other institutional settings.) Now, due to dwindling funds and a philosophical shift away from institutionalization, foster and adoptive families are living with and trying to contend with a worsening population of "transplanted" children.

Troubled Transplants: Unconventional Strategies for Helping Disturbed Foster and Adoptive Children addresses a gaping need for specific interventions with seriously troubled foster and adoptive children. These are children who arrive at the doorsteps of foster and adoptive families burdened with psychological "baggage."

This book was written for foster and adoptive families and for the professionals who work with them. It is an outgrowth of years of work with sensitive, talented and experienced foster and adoptive parents. Through our collective experience, we have discovered practical—if sometimes unconventional—treatment strategies for addressing the emotional/behavioral problems of these children and their disruptive influence on families. These strategies are employed with "troubled transplants" who require specialized interventions to stabilize their placements and to reduce their intransigent behavioral and emotional difficulties. Specialized treatment interventions spring from our understanding of the disturbed, formerly maltreated child and his impact on the foster and/or adoptive family.

The strategies outlined ahead are based upon a model of treatment whose core is "teamwork." It has been our experience that the essential treatment team consists of the foster/adoptive parents (and other family members), the birth parents (if still involved), the caseworker, mental health professional, school and others. Moreover, extensive clinical experience with disturbed children tells us that the key players on this the team are the foster or adoptive parents themselves.

(Note: For convenience sake, we will oftentimes refer to the foster/adoptive child as male. Also, to safeguard the privacy of children and families we have worked with, the cases described herein are fictionalized, disguised or are psychological composites. Any resemblance to actual, specific individuals is due to the sad fact that the traumatic histories and symptoms of maltreated children form a common, familiar mosaic.)

Overview of the Book

Chapter One describes the predicament in which many foster and adoptive parents find themselves: a disturbed child has been placed in their care, bringing with him uncanny ways of thwarting their attempts to help. In short order, caring, enthusiastic parents find themselves stymied, exasperated, exhausted and defeated by the child, his behavior problems and his maladaptive patterns of interacting in a family system.

In Chapter Two we focus on the maltreated—abused, neglected and/or sexually exploited—child. In placement, this child manifests a variety of characteristics, traits, behavior problems and disturbances. This chapter enumerates five categories of disturbed children commonly found in foster and adoptive placments and lists the hallmark signs or symptoms of each category. Following, we turn to a discussion of the child's mental blueprint of the world—his expectations about himself and caregivers in particular—which lies behind his behavior problems and symptoms. That mental blueprint has been sketched by the hand of chronic abuse, neglect and exploitation.

Chapter Three discusses the need for revising traditional theories about family systems. The chapter depicts and explains what happens to the family following the placement of a disturbed child in the home. Foster and adoptive family members can quickly fall prey to the child's negative mental blueprint—his cynical expectations about family life, intimacy and relationships.

In Chapter Four we address the need for unconventional treatment strategies with foster and adoptive children. These strategies target the unique psychopathology of the chronically maltreated child. We discuss the four central goals of treatment: containing acting-out behavior; increasing the child's verbalization; fostering negotiation skills; and promoting positive encounters with significant others.

Chapter Five presents eleven intervention strategies employed with disturbed foster and adoptive children. These strategies center upon the first two goals of treatment: containing acting-out behavior which threatens to sabotage the placement, and prompting the child to verbalize (rather than act-out) his feelings and negative mental blueprint of the world.

In Chapter Six we complete the presentation of intervention strategies—those which specifically address the third and fourth goals of treatment: namely, fostering negotiation skills (resolving differences and bargaining for the meeting of the child's needs by caregivers) and promoting positive encounters (close, intimate interactions).

Acknowledgements

We would like to thank the many foster and adoptive families who have both educated and worked together with us over the years. In addition, we wish to express our gratitude to those caseworkers and agency personnel who have collaborated with us and who have devoted themselves to helping disturbed children and their families. Our appreciation goes out to those who reviewed and offered insights during the preparation of this manuscript, namely: Dr. Vera Fahlberg, Tom Westfall, Sharon Thomas and Cora White. Thanks also to Helaine Hornby at the National Child Welfare Resource Center for her assistance in the publication of this book. Lastly, there are many distinguished professionals in our field who have stimulated and expanded our thinking: John Bowlby, Salvadore Minuchin, Milton Erickson, Carl Whitaker, Norman Polansky, Claudia Jewett, Vera Fahlberg, Selma Fraiberg, James Masterson, and Jay Haley. We lack sufficient words to acknowledge properly their contributions to the understanding of children and families.

Frank R. Kunstal
Richard J. Delaney

1993
Fort Collins, Colorado

To Our Wives

Miriam   and   Margaret

And To Our Children

Kirsten and Rachel   Katie and Claire

It is our lives with and love for them
that deepen our appreciation of families.

Frank R. Kunstal   Richard J. Delaney

Table of Contents

1 Introduction

While research reports the cost of child abuse to society in statistics and dollars and cents, the individual, human price is incalculable. Moreover, the powerful impact—negative and positive—of placing the disturbed, formerly maltreated child in a foster or adoptive family defies numerical description.

We begin with two woeful anecdotes: the first, a disrupted adoption; the second, an unsuccessful foster care placement. These anecdotes depict the unfortunate outcomes—the human cost—which follow when disturbed, abused/neglected/exploited children are unsuccessfully placed in caring homes.

A Troubled Adoption—An Introductory Anecdote

Turning to the first anecdote—that of a disrupted adoption—we see how the elements of parental inexperience, lack of support from professionals and agencies and sabotage by a seriously disturbed child combine to disrupt the placement permanently. (We should mention here that even experienced parents, those who have previously raised birth, foster or adoptive children, may succumb to the deleterious influence of the older disturbed child on their marriage and family. Children with histories of chronic maltreatment and/or loss of past caregivers present even talented, experienced adoptive parents with more than they bargained for.)

* * * * *

The adoptive parents skulked into the office tentatively. Mr. and Mrs.

1

Jones had aged visibly. In contrast to the excited, optimistic, confident parents prior to the placement of an older adopted child, they now were a crestfallen, defeated, bedraggled couple. As they talked, this couple—happily married before this ordeal—appeared strained, distant and blaming of each other. What had happened in the months following the adoption?

The Jones had no prior experience with children before the adoption. However, as an elementary school teacher Mrs. Jones felt assured that she could handle most children with ease. Mr. Jones, a businessman, competent breadwinner and solid citizen, felt equally confident.

Initially intending to adopt a healthy infant, the Jones found the adoption agency was soon inquiring about their interest in adopting a "special needs" child—an older child with deep emotional scars. At first they balked at the idea, having their hearts set on a baby. However, told that infant adoptions were hard to come by, Mr. and Mrs. Jones decided to consider the option of a sibling placement. In time they accepted an older boy with his infant sister. (They got their baby, but with an older child in tow!)

In short order, Crystal had attached to Mr. and Mrs. Jones. A six-month-old, she had been placed briefly in a foster home when her mother abandoned her and her older brother, Jason, age six. Crystal had been spared months and years of maltreatment and her capacity to attach to caregivers remained intact. However, Jason was not as fortunate, having endured years of neglect, abuse and sexual exploitation by his mother and a cavalcade of her boyfriends. In his earliest years he had been repeatedly placed outside the home following allegations of maltreatment. But, somehow he always found himself returned to the mother's "care." Typically, any changes on the mother's part were fleeting, with Jason again mistreated. A psychological evaluation ordered by the court when Jason was five-years-old (and in his ninth foster placement), portrayed him as "untrusting, depressive and withdrawn." It went on to say that he was a "manipulative, controlling and 'unattached' child, who felt the need to demand negative attention from parent figures."

In the Jones' adoptive home, Jason was passive, withdrawn and avoidant. He never smiled and was unable to say what he was upset about. However, signs of his anger emerged and he was "insanely jealous" of any attention shown towards his baby sister. When Mrs. Jones included Jason in some "taking care of baby" activities, she found him dangerously rough with Crystal. In addition, when he was left alone with her, Crystal always cried and once was found with a large red mark across her face. Though Jason staunchly denied it, the mark appeared to be his handprint.

Whenever Mrs. Jones attempted to reach out to Jason, he rebuffed her. For example, if she embraced him he stiffened like a board and pulled away from her. If she spoke kindly to him, he paid no attention. When she complimented him on his artwork, he immediately tore up the paper. In a word, Jason was unreachable.

Even more unsettling to Mrs. Jones than the cold shoulder from Jason was the rage he provoked in her. Everything was a power struggle with him. If she asked him to put on his clothes, he tore them in the process. If she turned her back on him for a moment, he sneaked food from the refrigerator. When Mrs. Jones bottle-fed or diapered Crystal, Jason acted out his smoldering jealousy in silent revenge. Once, for instance, while she was ministering to a sick Crystal, Jason deliberately broke the thermometer and poured the baby medicine down the drain.

In contrast to his wife's increasing exasperation, Mr. Jones experienced Jason—early in the adoption—as a "typical boy." He described his evenings with Jason as follows: "When I get home at night he runs into my arms with 'Daddy! Daddy!'" When his wife gave harrowing accounts of life with Jason, Mr. Jones at first attributed it to "new mother's jitters." He tried to reassure her, but she accused him of "patronizing" her. A widening chasm grew between the couple for the first time in their marriage. All-the-while, Jason's problems worsened with his adoptive mother. He began stealing from her and, though never defying her openly, he refused to comply with anything she asked. Whenever Mrs. Jones attempted to hold or sit with him, Jason squirmed away or embraced her in what she described as "phoney, wet-noodle hugs."

As the situation deteriorated at the Jones' home, the adoption agency paid an emergency visit and assessed the situation as follows: "This first time mother seems to overreact to the child's minor behavior problems... Mrs. Jones appears to be less 'motherly' than the home study determined...During the home visit she seemed quite distant from Jason and never invited him to sit by her. There was very little eye contact between them...Mr. Jones seemed to be the primary parent, and Jason has begun to form a healthy attachment to him. Mr. Jones comes across as much more stable, warm and available than his wife...appears to be deep disagreement between the couple about Jason's personality...marital communication is quite strained." The adoption worker recommended individual psychotherapy for the child to help with adjustment, "supportive counseling" for Mrs. Jones, and marital counseling for the couple to resolve wide differences in perception and management of Jason in the home.

Despite three months of counseling, the problem had worsened measurably: Jason's acting-out towards the adoptive mother had increased; Mrs. Jones had become completely disenchanted, felt misunderstood and blamed, and suggested to her husband that they might need to give Jason back. Mr. Jones expressed his disbelief in his wife's strong reaction and in her complaints about Jason. However, the stress of poor marital communication and growing disagreements with his wife had begun to take a toll on him as well. He had developed a sleep disturbance and complained of frequent "heartburn." Throughout all of this storm and stress, both parents had developed a deep attachment to Crystal, who was a delightful, bubbly, rewarding baby. Mrs. Jones stated that her love of Crystal kept her trying with Jason (out of fear of losing Crystal, if Jason's adoption failed).

At about this time, Jason's psychotherapist wrote to the adoption agency, stating that the relationship between Mrs. Jones and Jason was the source of Jason's on-going difficulties. He related that Jason had the "capacity to bond" and was a "highly adoptable" boy who had been placed with the wrong family. Though he admitted to having minimal contact with either adoptive parent, the therapist emphatically recommended that the adoption agency remove both children from the Jones family as soon as possible. Above the protests of the parents, the children were removed abruptly and placed with another adoptive family.

* * * * *

Commentary

> *"All too frequently, parents adopt, poorly prepared and under-supported."*

This tragic tale of adoption disruption chronicles an all too common occurrence in "special needs" adoptions. The Jones family and Jason (and to a lesser extent, Crystal) are the subjects of this book. We will focus herein on these "troubled transplants"— emotionally disturbed, formerly maltreated children who destabilize in placement—foster or adoptive. Thankfully, not all such cases end in the ultimate demise of the family and the placement.

All too frequently parents adopt, poorly prepared and under-supported. They often complain later about the limited information on the child, his diagnosis, behavioral problems and history of abuse, neglect and exploitation. Although some adoptive parents concede that they had been warned of problems and had been advised to follow-up on counseling for themselves and their adoptive child, many put it off until too late. Without assistance, many adoptive parents are overwhelmed by the seriousness of the problematical children in their home. In short order, they find the relative tranquility of their families disturbed by negative forces. From within, they find that the child plays a divisive, unsettling role in the family. The child's pattern of emotional and behavioral problems disrupt normal marital and family functioning and evoke strong, disquieting feelings in the parents and in other children in the home. From without, they feel unsupported, blamed, scapegoated and punished—by professionals, agencies, and individuals who are in the position to help—for the child's on-going problems.

A Troubled Foster Placement—A Second Anecdote

Parents who adopt disturbed children are not the only ones beseiged by the vicissitudes of caregiving. Foster home and group home parents also may rapidly find themselves in domestic distress, following the placement of a troubled foster child, as we will see in the second anecdote.

* * * * *

Mr. and Mrs. Miller, a semi-retired farm couple, were seasoned foster parents, having worked with a wide range of children and adolescents throughout their fifteen years of service. Their four natural children were all grown and gone, and the Miller's believed that they could provide a good home for less fortunate children; and they were right. Numerous children had benefitted from their loving, firm parenting.

Now the Millers were well aware, through their own experience, that the problems presented by foster kids had seemed to worsen over the years. Indeed, they had witnessed an increase in how disturbed these abused and neglected children were; the Millers reported that almost all of their foster children had not only been physically abused and neglected, but also sexually abused. Despite their invaluable years of experience, the Millers were unprepared for Thelma, their latest—and ultimately last—foster child.

Thelma, age eleven, was "hell-on-wheels," according to the Miller's. Newly released from the state mental hospital, she had been "through the mill." Mrs. Miller, who did most of the foster parenting, described Thelma this way: "She is a bizarre kid—a Dr. Jekyl and Mrs. Hyde. Her birth mom was on drugs when she was pregnant with her. Thelma doesn't remember her, though." The biological mother, a prostitute, may have let her "clientele" sexually assault Thelma, when she was still a toddler. Thelma had her first case of gonnorhea at the age of twenty-eight months. Reports of neglect deluged the child welfare department; and Thelma was finally removed and placed in a "kinship" foster home with a maternal aunt. Sadly, this woman was neglectful and inadequate and seemingly unphased by Thelma's sexual involvement with older neighborhood boys. Eventually, when Thelma's late-nite sexual escapades interrupted the aunt's sleep, she gave the child to the maternal grandmother, who raised her out of duty. Predictably, Thelma was too much for the grandmother, who gave her to the "system." A series of foster home placements followed, since Thelma's behavior problems undermined placements one-by-one. In addition to sexual acting-out, Thelma had become self-mutilating and periodically suicidal. When frustrated, Thelma would bang her head against the wall or floor, and she left bite marks up and down her arms. One evening, she got up in the night, turned on the stove's gas burners and placed unopened cans of pop on them. Her foster parents awakened to the sound of exploding cans. At that point, Thelma was placed for six weeks in the state hospital, as her erratic, dangerous behavior alarmed the foster parents and caseworker.

By the time the Miller's took Thelma into their home, she had lived with multiple relatives, in ten foster homes, and—most recently—a state psychiatric hospital. Each successive foster home reported an increasing number of behavioral problems, ranging from bedwetting to head-banging and from compulsive stealing to chronic masturbation. Although her most dangerous behavior had been "stabilized" during her hospitalization, Thelma remained an unlikeable, disturbed, frighteningly jealous child who kept the Miller family stirred up. When she was around, other children fought with her and each other—constantly. Thelma was a quietly angry, rage-filled child who provoked others to express the anger she held in check. She rarely, if ever, vocalized any anger directly to adults, but engaged in unending, spiteful power struggles with them. For example, when asked at the dinner table to eat a small portion of a vegetable that she disliked, Thelma regurgitated on her plate and smeared it on the table cloth.

Thelma's chronic masturbation and seduction of her peers was not totally unexpected by the foster parents, who had dealt with this problem in past placements. However, Thelma's sexual activity with the family pets and farm animals was quite appalling and unacceptable to the Miller's. Although they had heard of bestiality in the past, none of their foster children had exhibited that behavior. When they found Thelma directing other foster children to fellate the family dog, the Millers asked that she be removed from their home, feeling that they could not *adequately supervise her around the farm.*

* * * * *

A Commentary

Today's foster parents are called upon to care for extremely disturbed children. Indeed, gone are the days when foster parents would care for psychologically "normal" children whose mother was hospitalized briefly or children who were suddenly orphaned. Indeed, the lion's share of today's foster children have been sorely abused, neglected, and sexually exploited—boys and girls alike. Most foster parents are asked to provide much more than a sound family

"Most foster parents are asked to provide much more than a sound family environment."

environment. "Therapeutic" agents by necessity, they must provide a "treatment milieu" for children suffering from conduct disorders, clinical depression, separation anxiety, childhood schizophrenia, fetal alcohol syndrome, mental retardation, attention deficit disorder, seizure disorders, and many other daunting medical/psychiatric maladies. These children, in years past, would have been placed in psychiatric hospitals or residential treatment centers. Currently, due to limited funding and to a philosophical shift in how we treat children, many reside in family rather than institutional settings. Many other children, recently discharged from hospitals and treatment centers, are placed immediately into foster homes. In many instances, these children are "right on the edge" of a mandatory inpatient stay; but they remain in the foster home, where we affix undersized psychic band-aids to gaping emotional wounds.

Concluding Remarks

The underlying premise of this book is that the family—foster or adoptive—contains the key ingredients for change in the disturbed child. Sadly, while the significance of the foster or adoptive family to the seriously troubled child is theoretically acknowledged, these families are routinely overlooked or exiled from treatment. All too often, foster and adoptive families are passive spectators. These families seldom receive credit for the child's gains, though frequently they take the blame for the child's failures. Ironically, helping professionals often miss the significance of the unhealthy, abusive histories these "troubled transplants" bring into the foster or adoptive home. As an outgrowth of this omission, the child's difficulties are seen as "rooted" in presumably disturbed foster or adoptive family dynamics. This is particularly easy for the professional to justify, if the foster or adoptive family appears troubled and distressed, as is common in such placements. However, even when the family and the marital couple is not observably troubled, professionals scrutinize the family for suspect, hidden, insidious problems. In either case the family cannot win. And in the end, the child loses as well.

2 The Maltreated Child

This chapter will focus on the maltreated child—the child most often seen in foster homes and in special needs adoptions. This child has been the victim of abuse, neglect and exploitation and has been involved in the "system" as a ward of the state.

The history of maltreatment by earlier caregivers along with subsequent experience of "drifting" through a series of foster placements does immeasurable damage to the child's mental health. Among other things, the maltreated child has developed a limited capacity to relate genuinely to others, to behave age-appropriately, to empathize, to feel guilt or remorse, to grow attached and to control his aggressive impulses. The child has developed a perception of the world in general, and of parent figures in particular, which is remarkably jaded and cynical. He expects—based upon his own history of abuse, neglect, abandonment, rejection and loss—that caregivers are not to be counted upon and that he must fend for himself. This leaves him feeling insecure, apprehensive and wary about the world.

In this chapter we begin with case histories of maltreated children and follow with a discussion of five common categories of disturbed youngsters found in foster and adoptive care: the antisocial, overanxious/insecure, withdrawn/asocial, inadequate/dependent, and mixed type. Next, we describe the negative mental blueprint, or cynical view of the world, which underlies the maltreated child's typical behavior problems. The negative mental blueprint is illustrated graphically by vivid drawings completed by "troubled transplants"—disturbed foster and adoptive children.

Case Histories

Let us turn now to two cases which illustrate the destructive effects of maltreatment on children:

* * * * *

Veronica had been through 21 foster homes by the age of nine, when she was adopted. After six long months, the disillusioned adoptive parents gave her up because of her emotional withdrawal, firesetting, urinating down the heat ducts and seductiveness. Interestingly, the adoptive parents reported that Veronica never expressed any feelings of dissatisfaction with them or their home. Indeed, they stated that Veronica had never, never, voiced any anger, frustration, or difference of opinion in all the months she had lived with them. They added that she was always compliant and pleasant; and she never argued, protested or disagreed with them as did their younger biological children. From that standpoint, they maintained that she was a "model child," though gradually they came to see her as telling them what they wanted to hear, while "she would go off and set a fire somewhere. . . .We never had any clue that she was upset or mad about anything, and then we'd smell smoke again." Veronica's early history revealed that she had been severely, sadistically abused by a stepfather who had repeatedly beaten her with objects, had thrown her against the wall head first, and had tied her to the toilet in a dark bathroom for wetting her pants.

* * * * *

Bobby was eleven at the time of his second try at adoption. Although he had been severely sexually abused by his biological mother, father and older siblings when he was a preschooler, the greatest emotional scars were left by horrendous deprivation. Bobby had been a failure-to-thrive baby whose family was frequently reported to the child protection agency for lack of supervision, for failure to return to the doctor's office for follow-up on his growth problem, and for raising him and two other children in utter filth—including animal feces on the carpet, fermenting garbage in the sink, and trash heaped in every room. As a three-year-old, Bobby was left alone for an entire weekend while his parents disappeared out-of-state. Neighbors reported him to the authorities after he was found eating out of garbage cans when he was age five. A thoroughly "street-wise" kid at age ten, Bobby lived with older teen-aged runaways for days at a time, sneaking home to steal food and money while his parents were out carousing. After placement in shelter care, a group home and a residential child care facility, Bobby was deemed ready for adoption. However, as might be expected, after eight months in a family the adoptive "experiment" failed.

* * * * *

As in the cases above, many if not most special needs adoptive (and emotionally disturbed foster) children have been exposed to chronic abuse, neglect and/or sexual exploitation in the months and years before placement into a foster or adoptive home. This history of maltreatment has almost inevitably damaged the child at a deep level psychologically. In the case of Veronica above, early repeated abuse was the chief damaging factor. Veronica had learned to survive in a dangerous world where parent figures would erupt violently and abusively towards her at any moment. She in short order learned to adapt to a highly volatile, dysfunctional family system. As a result, as with many abused children, she became—around the adult world—hypervigilant, isolated and almost wooden in appearance. She rarely, if ever, voiced her own feelings, needs, frustrations, or conflicts around her parents, as that might have invited more abuse. Instead she "stuffed" those feelings and developed "emotional radar" which equipped her to pick up on the nuances in the moods of adults around her—are they mad, happy, sad or are they imminently dangerous? While wearing plastered-on smiles, in reality Veronica had become an emotionally flat, joyless, "simulated child"—a two-dimensional caricature of a living, breathing youngster. She had learned to adapt to the moods and personalities around her, and in so doing, became a "chameleon-like" child.

In the case of Bobby, he had learned to avoid the adult world by taking care of his needs himself or by turning to other ragamuffin, "feral" children for help. Bobby lacked the incendiary anger of the fire-setting Veronica. However, his thorough withdrawal from adult caregivers had a chilling effect on his placement. Some children who have received little early-on in life, have little to give once placed. They remain unmoved and untouched by family life.

Characteristics of the Chronically Maltreated Child

Maltreated children evidence a host of interpersonal problems: fears, anxieties, mistrust towards adults, bottomless needs, anger, ambivalence, resistance, impulsive self-damaging behavior, withdrawal from normal childhood activities, and a certain pessimism about life.

The maltreatment which these children have suffered at the hands of parent figures or other adults often destroys any feelings of trust in caregivers. Indeed, these youngsters always keep one eye open around all caregivers, whether caseworker, therapist, foster or adoptive parent. Having been "objectified"— treated as a "thing" by the adult world — they have grown to expect that their own personal needs, feelings and opinions are inconsequential. In their reality, it was the need of the adult that took prominence. Consequently, the essential need of the child to remain a protected, unmolested, joyful, developing being was grossly devalued.

We have discovered in our clinical work that there are several types of maltreated children found in foster and adoptive homes.[1] Abused, neglected and exploited children vary in how disturbed they are and what their behavior problems are, and they differ in the specific characteristics which they show after such maltreatment. An increasing number of children in foster and adoptive placements are "severely disturbed." When they have been victims of chronic maltreatment, they often fall into one of five categories (see Table 2.1). The differences in these children may relate to the innate temperament, the extent of the maltreatment, the nature of the attachments to caregivers, and the frequency and nature of disruptions in early caregiving.

Table 2.1 Five Categories of Seriously Disturbed Children

- Antisocial Type
- Overanxious/Insecure Type
- Withdrawn/Asocial Type
- Inadequate/Dependent Type
- Mixed Type

We will now turn to a discussion of the five categories of children seen in foster and adoptive work. (Note: as you might expect, not all children fall neatly into one of the five categories. That is, there is often overlap. Also, within each category children can vary in terms of severity of disturbance.)

Five Categories of Disturbed Children in Foster/Adoptive Care

The Antisocial Type

The category very commonly associated with the disturbed, maltreated child is the antisocial type. These children have been depicted variously as conduct-disordered, undersocialized aggressive reaction, sociopathic, delinquent, character-disordered, or "unattached." Antisocial foster or adoptive children manifest a typical pattern of symptoms, some of which are seen in the case of Sid below:

* * * * *

After his third foster home, Sid, age thirteen, had become unmanageable. Even a residential child care facility was unable to handle him at first. In fact, he was dubbed "Sid Vicious" by the staff. This boy, though only thirteen years of age, was uncontrollably angry and combative. He had assaulted a female staff member with a knife stolen from the kitchen. She had fortunately surprised both herself and Sid by disarming him. Other children reported to the staff that Sid was climbing out of his bedroom window at night. When the staff lay in wait for him the next evening, they found the boy climbing up the downspout to the girls' quarters. It eventually became clear that Sid had been sexually active with some of the older girls and with some of the younger boys in the treatment center, continuing the sexual acting-out he had done in foster homes earlier-on. Sid had extorted sexual favors and promises of silence from his many victims by threats of physical violence.

* * * * *

In the case of "Sid Vicious" above, we find a boy who had been heinously physically abused and ritualistically sexually abused by both his mother and father. This excessive maltreatment twisted Sid into a malicious boy with an abnormal connection to other human beings—a "hollow child" without compassion for his fellow man; the very fiber of his being was pessimistic and cynical, and he viewed the world with a jaundiced eye.

Antisocial foster and adoptive children similar to Sid have problems ranging from cruelty to animals and children, to firesetting, to indiscriminate attachments to others. Table 2.2 lists the hallmark signs of this category of maltreated child.

(It should be pointed out here that not all antisocial foster and adoptive children are as decidedly disturbed as Sid, nor do they manifest as many of the aggressive, assaultive and coercive sexual behaviors as he did. As a matter of fact, many antisocial children show a very winsome, charming and charismatic quality which makes them initially quite appealing to others. They can be non-violent and overtly compliant, though eventually they are found to be quite passive-aggressive, manipulative and secretly resentful and untrusting. Though such children fail to present the obvious dangers and challenges of a boy like Sid, they can wreck havoc on the foster or adoptive home in other, more subtle ways.)

Table 2.2 Hallmark Signs of Antisocial Children

- Sadism/violence.
- Disordered eating.
- Counterfeit emotionality.
- Kleptomania/compulsive lying.
- Sexual obsessions.
- Passive-aggression.
- Defective conscience.
- Oppositionality, resistance, defiance and controlling behavior.

The Overanxious/Insecure Type

The second category of disturbed children seen in foster and adoptive care is the overanxious/insecure type. These children have been diagnosed as cases of separation anxiety, school phobia or overanxious attachment. Overanxious/insecure foster or adoptive children manifest a number of clear-cut symptoms (see Table 2.3), as seen in the following case of "Ricky":

* * * * *

Ricky, a frail eight-year-old Caucasian boy, was agitated and anxious in the first interview—an emergency session following his sudden placement into a receiving home. Ricky had been abandoned again by his mother, a chronic paranoid schizophrenic who deserted him on a downtown street in a large metropolitan city. Ricky and his mother were among the growing ranks of homeless. His mother occasionally prostituted, then quickly spent any income on alcohol. When inebriated she was more erratic than ever. It was on such an occasion that she left Ricky—screaming that she would kill him because he was on "their side"—whoever "they" were.

Once in placement, according to the foster mother, Ricky never left her side, shadowing her every move. He was unable to shut the door to the bathroom when he had to go, for fear of being alone. She reported that he would wet all over himself because he "ran in place" nervously as he urinated. In addition, the foster mother commented that Ricky, while all the rest of the foster family watched television, would sit and stare eerily into her eyes.

Among Ricky's many problems in foster care were the following: fear of sleeping alone in a room without a light on; inability to play by himself or occupy himself; fears about his birth mother dying; and regular nightmares about monsters, losing his mother and death.

* * * * *

Overanxious/insecure children like Ricky are commonly highly apprehensive and insecure. They often manifest pure panic about separations from their caregivers. They show few of the signs of anti-social category, but rather demonstrate problems of their own, such as school avoidance, night fears and obsessions about losing a parent. However, there are some children who fit this category but show much more ambivalence towards their caregivers — a love-hate relationship.

Interestingly, during the course of Ricky's foster and later adoptive placement, the source of his anxieties became clear. He had been chronically abandoned, deserted and oftentimes physically abused by his birth mother. Intermittently between desertions and beatings she insisted on a symbiotic relationship with him. A woman with massive fears of just about everything, she was unable to function alone for long. Ricky during those times, was her constant companion in the house, on errands and even in bed. When the young child's companionship failed to allay her anxieties, this woman would abuse alcohol (and sometimes drugs) and would—on a "bender"—disappear for days or weeks at a time. On occasion, this desperate, seriously mentally ill woman would bring home strange men who would temporarily evict Ricky from his mother's bedroom.

Table 2.3. Hallmark Signs of Overanxious/Insecure Children

- School avoidance.
- Night fears.
- Obsessions about losing a parent.
- Fear of being alone.
- Depression when separated.
- Worries about sickness, injury, death.
- Nightmares with separation and loss themes.
- Ambivalent, intense love-hate feelings towards caregivers.

The Withdrawn/Asocial Type

In sharp contrast to the overanxious/insecure child, withdrawn/asocial foster and adoptive children show a remarkable lack of anxiety about their isolation from others (see Table 2.4). In fact, they effectively and resolutely insulate themselves from outsiders. They seem "comfortable" in their aloneness, wherein they hide from the pain of interpersonal complexities. Thick emotional buffers cushion them from the hurt of intimacy, the agony of separation and loss, as we see in the following case:

* * * * *

Penny, age seven, shuffled down the hallway to the therapy room. Her shoulders were sloped, her arms dangled limply and she wore a dreary expression on her face. Once in the room she spoke only when spoken to—her eyes downcast. When eye contact was requested by the therapist, Penny briefly directed her unfocused gaze in the general vicinity of his voice. She never volunteered any personal information. Many of the examiner's questions or comments were followed by monosyllabic answers or by total silence. If this child felt any emotion, it was concealed behind a mask of indifference. Penny's "hidden agenda" was to discourage interaction at all costs. Hers was a thoroughly intransigent avoidance of the adult world. Of note was her response to a previous psychotherapist who had attempted "rage therapy"—an intrusive, often highly effective psychotherapeutic approach which evokes submerged anger from the child. To this approach Penny was utterly unresponsive. Even after a two hour tickling session, she failed to respond. It merely drove her into a deeper withdrawal.

* * * * *

Many disturbed foster or adoptive children are markedly withdrawn, isolated and avoidant around other human beings. They are interpersonally detached and may actively or passively spurn close human relationships due to their deep distrust. Socially inept, they are shunned by other children. Unable to empathize accurately, they simply do not understand the feelings of others. They are often emotionally blunted and psychologically impoverished.

Penny was the product of a rape and had been raised in a chronically neglectful home by her depressed mother. As a toddler, she was given "custodial" care by her mother; that is, Penny was kept alive physically. However, she had never received one iota of maternal warmth. Indeed, her mother was a caustic, rejecting, icy woman who never stopped pointing out to the child that she was unwelcome and unwanted. In desperation, Penny turned to a family dog for companionship and solace.

Table 2.4 Hallmark Signs of Withdrawn/Asocial Children

- Glaring defects in the capacity for developing relationships.
- Lack of social hunger.
- Unconcern about isolation from others.
- Few apparent needs for affection or emotional attachments.
- Lack of spontaneous emotional expression.
- Obliviousness to others and lack of insight.

The Inadequate/Dependent Type

By contrast to the withdrawn/asocial child, inadequate/dependent children are clinging vines who latch onto caregivers and exhaust them with bottomless needs. They differ from overanxious/insecure children in that they cling to almost anyone instantly and yet are often only superficially connected or attached to those that they "glom onto," as seen in the case of "Kara."

* * * * *

Kara, an overweight six-year-old adopted girl, was "draining" the adoptive mother dry. "I can't really put my finger on it," this beleaguered woman commented, "She takes and takes all day long in little ways, and she gives nothing in return." Kara never stopped asking for her needs to be met, chattering absently and constantly, and relentlessly posing questions to her adoptive mother. Kara seemed helpless and hopeless, unable to do anything for herself. For example, she would sit in her bedroom before breakfast without moving, until the adoptive mother would physically push her in the direction of the clothes closet. In general, Kara was completely docile, submissive and non-assertive around the other youngsters in the home. She continuously whined and tattled on the other children, who eventually came to victimize her. Kara never entertained herself, looking to the adoptive mother to direct her every move.

* * * * *

Disturbed foster or adoptive children who are inadequate and dependent show hallmark signs which are summarized in Table 2.5. These children are excessively needy and emotionally stunted. That is, they require guidance, holding and constant attention. They often are defenseless against other children, leaning on the parent to stand up for them. In addition, they have little confidence in themselves, always turning to the adult for guidance. They may be submissive to others and may never show any sign of rebellion or difference of opinion. There is virtually no interest in "mastery," independence, or maturity.

Table 2.5 Hallmark Signs of Inadequate/Dependent Children

- Insatiable neediness.
- Submissiveness.
- Learned helplessness and low self-esteem.
- Lack of interest in mastering the environment.
- Flatness of emotion; lack of vitality.
- Apathy-futility; massive emotional voids.

The question might be raised again here: How do these children differ from the withdrawn/asocial category described earlier? In response, we would point out how Kara's adoptive mother described her: "Kara would sit on my lap all night and day. . .for that matter, she'd sit on almost anyone's lap. . .it wouldn't really matter whose lap." Our distinction between the withdrawn child and the inadequate/dependent child is in the contact which the latter child allows—or more accurately—seeks out ravenously from nearly any other human. Further, the movement of the inadequate/dependent child is towards people, no matter how meaningless and superficial the contact; whereas, with the withdrawn/asocial child, movement is clearly away from other humans.

The Mixed Type

There are particular children who defy categorization. These children have a wide variety of behavioral and interpersonal problems and seldom show a dominant trait or set of traits. Though they clearly appear seriously disturbed, their problems are perplexing, enigmatic and difficult to predict. They manifest a variety of specific and seemingly unrelated symptoms (see Table 2.6), as seen in the following case:

* * * * *

William was separated from his much younger brother and placed in foster care due to his brutal assaults on him. In one dramatic display of temper, William had smashed his metal "John Deere" tractor into his brother's face, driving his teeth through his lips. William had learned to hit and hurt from his own experiences: from a mother who expected this young boy to be "the man of the house" in his father's absence, leading her to place unrealistic demands on him, and to be in an angry role-inversion which at times was rife with sexual innuendo. At the same time, she babied her younger son, "the good one," affectionate and protective of him. Her cuddling would incense William, who would later get back at his brother. William's typical punishment, as his mother believed in "an eye for an eye," was a series of ten slaps to the face (one for each year of his age). This infuriated William all-the-more, though his response was to appease his then withdrawing mother.

Although his family was "intact," William's father was an over-the-road trucker who was gone for several weeks at a stretch. When he did make his brief returns home, he fought with the mother constantly, their altercations only momentarily punctuated by harsh discipline of the boys. When a neighbor threatened to report the family after seeing William forced to sleep in the cold cab of the truck, the parents abruptly decided to pick up and move, leaving William with relatives. When days turned into weeks without any contact from the parents, they contacted the welfare agency and William was placed in protective care.

In his foster placement William was an angry, red-faced, "psychological menagerie." When unsupervised he was vicious, aggressive and hurtful to the younger children. He seemed to sense the foster mother's presence with "feelers," and when she was around he would insist on her attention, wanting to be with her for hours at a time. William loved to act like a baby, and a mean one at that.

When accidentally bumped while playing, or when not getting his way, he would briefly tantrum, then isolate himself in his room. At times, especially when frustrated, William would turn "beet red" with anger, while crying and wanting affection. The foster mother quipped that they had in placement "the many faces of William," as she did not know which William she should be responding to. At various times he was playmate, infant, meddler, hermit, controller and appendage. When the foster parents enrolled him in the child outpatient program at a nearby teaching hospital, William was a diagnostic "dream come true" for the psychiatric residents. In short order he had diagnoses ranging from "multiple personality disorder," to "post-traumatic stress disorder," to "funny looking kid."

Rejected and displaced, having had little success in "fitting in," William was an internal "hodgepodge" of needs and demands, and he could change his character in a moment. Over time and with stable and caring foster placement, William settled down and showed himself to be the child he really was: a needy, dependent youngster with much anxiety and insecurity.

* * * * *

While no disturbed child fits precisely into a particular category, most troubled children typically have "hallmark" symptoms and behaviors which define their overall personality. When no personality pattern rises to the surface as dominant, these children are categorized as "mixed."

Table 2.6 Hallmark Signs of Mixed Type Child

- A lack of dominant, hallmark behavior problems and characteristics.
- A changeable, unstable manner of relating to others.
- Widely varying needs and demands.
- An active, shifting emotional state.

The Mental Blueprint

The behavior problems, signs and symptoms of disturbed children in foster and adoptive homes are at times baffling, especially when taken out-of-context—the context being who the child is, how he has been raised, what he expects from others and how he views his world. We will see next that the maltreated child's view of the world is skewed. Indeed, the maltreatment of the young child leaves more than physical wounds. There are invisible scars to the child's personality development and incalculable damage to his sense of trust, empathy, confidence and security. Along with that comes the negative impact upon the child's view of the world, upon his "mental blueprint" of the way that people relate to each other.

In the early months and years of life, the child develops a set of expectations about the world and individuals around him. A child who has been treated well expects to be kept safe, to be treated sensitively, and to be allowed to express feelings and needs. Given "good enough" parenting and an average infant, toddler or young child, the resultant mental blueprint is a hopeful sketch of the world and caregivers, parent figures and others. By contrast, the chronically maltreated child expects anything but good treatment. His view of relationships is colored by months and years of insensitive, erratic, unavailable and pain-inflicting parenting. His expectations are highly suspicious and pessimistic, and he ultimately develops a mental "black-and-blueprint" of the world and caregivers (see Table 2.7).

Table 2.7 The Mental Blueprint of the Maltreated Child

About himself:

I am WORTHLESS.
I am UNSAFE.
I am WEAK.

About caregivers:

They are UNRESPONSIVE.
They are UNRELIABLE.
They are DANGEROUS.

The contents of the maltreated child's mental blueprint are cynical and hopeless. Specifically, the child views himself as worthless, unsafe and weak, while caregivers are perceived as unresponsive, unreliable and dangerous. Based upon these perceptions, the child behaves in predictable ways, some of which have been survival-enhancing in the past: for example, withdrawing or removing himself from close contact with his parents and avoiding any disclosure of thoughts and feelings which the adults might find offensive or negative. Unfortunately, even after the child is removed from the abusive, neglectful, exploitive environment and is placed in a nurturing, caring foster or adoptive home, his mental blueprint persists. Consequently, behavior problems—which reflect the underlying mental blueprint—continue or even worsen in the new home, much to the chagrin of the foster or adoptive family. Characteristically, the maltreated child views the surrogate family through distorted lenses. And, through a twisted metamorphosis, the unsuspecting, caring foster/adoptive caregivers are perceived and experienced by the child as the abusive, neglectful, exploitive parents from his past.

Maltreated children convey to us their mental blueprint of the world through what they say, what they fail to say and through what they do and don't do. The child for instance, who describes other children as "sneaky, mean or unfair," and who jealously declares his possessions "off limits," may in reality be telling us about his past experiences with others who were stingy with him. Certainly, the child who states of his father, "Well, he doesn't beat us as much as he used to," is revealing the state of family life and his perception of his father figure. Some children discard their possessions, lose what is given to them, or in some way set themselves up to be deprived—possible symbols of the sense of "worthlessness" they feel. The child who sneaks, hides or gorges food is demonstrating the deprivation he has experienced.

As we will see in the following chapters, a central goal of treatment of disturbed children is to elicit from them their underlying perceptions, beliefs, feelings about and views of the world—their mental blueprint. This eliciting is crucial to understanding what lies behind the child's often inexplicable behavior problems. In many of these children, the invisible wounds from early maltreatment fester under the surface and later ooze out and contaminate later relationships. The mental blueprint functions as the receptacle of those unseen, festering wounds.

In our evaluation and treatment of disturbed foster/adoptive children, there are several ways by which we uncover or observe the mental blueprint. In clinical practice, we gather information about it through knowledge of his history of maltreatment and family relationships, through observation of his behavior problems, through a study of his relationships in the foster or adoptive home, through his symbolic play, through what he says, and—interestingly—even through his art work. Throughout our discussion of cases in this book, we will often allude to the child's history, earliest relationships, behavior problems, verbalizations, and relationships in the foster and adoptive home. However, at this point, we would like to focus very specifically on drawings done by disturbed foster and adoptive children.

We have found in our work that drawings produced by maltreated children provide at times "graphic" illustrations of how the child views his world, his caregivers and himself. Though we do not rely exclusively on drawings for the purpose of diagnosis, we do incorporate them with what is gleaned from other sources. Let us now turn to an examination and discussion of drawings produced by abused, neglected, exploited children seen in foster and adoptive homes.

Children's Drawings

Drawing A was sketched by Donny, a nine-year-old adopted boy from Viet Nam. This boy's adoptive placement was in jeopardy due to his explosive, angry assaults towards younger children in the home, to his habitual theft of objects from around the house, and to his total lack of relationship to his adoptive mother. His art work was produced in response to a request for a picture of a "non-existing animal" (NEA), that is, a creature that he would have to create from his imagination. After he finished this drawing, Donny explained that this was an extinct dinosaur, a harmless plant-eater that would run from meat-eaters and escape into a large body of water, where the Tyranasaurus Rex (a meat-eater) could not follow. Striking in this drawing was his emphasis on the dinosaur's chest, which Donny described as large breasts. This emphasis was original and significant with the breast development symbolically suggesting Donny's unmet dependency, the need for nurturance, and the desire to be mothered. His choice of a harmless, passive, though immense, creature provides us clues about how Donny views himself. Despite his, at times, aggressive behavior in the adoptive home, he is lacking in any "attack capabilities" and the ability to protect

Drawing A

himself, an overgrown, harmless "Baby Huey." In particular, Donny felt defenseless around adult caregivers.

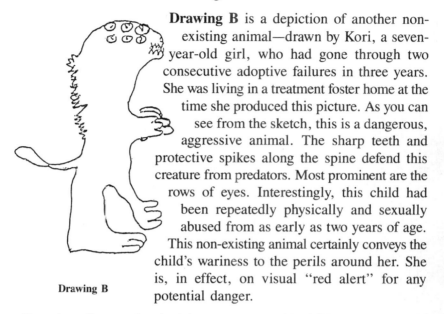

Drawing B is a depiction of another non-existing animal—drawn by Kori, a seven-year-old girl, who had gone through two consecutive adoptive failures in three years. She was living in a treatment foster home at the time she produced this picture. As you can see from the sketch, this is a dangerous, aggressive animal. The sharp teeth and protective spikes along the spine defend this creature from predators. Most prominent are the rows of eyes. Interestingly, this child had been repeatedly physically and sexually abused from as early as two years of age. This non-existing animal certainly conveys the child's wariness to the perils around her. She is, in effect, on visual "red alert" for any potential danger.

Drawing B

Drawing C was sketched by a ten-year-old child who had been repeatedly sodomized by his older stepbrothers. His neglectful, single mother had been abusing street drugs and had failed to provide protection or supervision of her children. This boy's stark portrayal of the NEA is replete with phallic symbols—note especially the two serpentine shapes

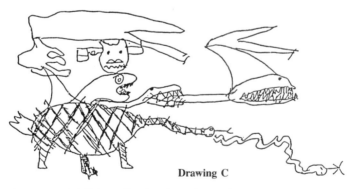

Drawing C

at the bottom. Additionally, he described the three heads in the center of the picture, as follows: "This is an animal that keeps coming at you with his sharp teeth...when you run away from it, it reaches out to you with another head, which stretches towards you as far as you can run...When it can't go any further...another head comes out and stretches for you—you can never get away from it." This poignant verbal description, along with the drawing, speaks to this boy's helplessness against the abuse. It summarizes his perception of the world as perilous and himself as impotent and victimized. Ironically, in foster care, he seemed to provoke more abuse from others, and he was, in the foster mother's words, "the perfect victim."

Drawing D by a seriously disturbed foster boy shows an ominous character with frightening glare and threatening posture and suggests this teenager's preoccupation with satanic themes. Oddly, this boy—on the surface—was an extremely compliant, timid and withdrawn foster child who presented no behavior problems in the home. However his fantasy world, expressed in drawings, doodlings and essays at school, grew increasingly bizarre and rage-filled. The alarmed teachers informed the foster parents about his apparent mental deterioration. This child, who had been horribly neglected from the time he was a toddler, was ultimately placed in a psychiatric hospital where he was stabilized, medicated with anti-psychotic drugs, and then returned to the treatment foster home. While hospitalized he revealed a history of ritualistic sexual abuse.

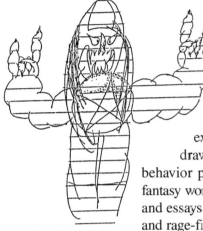

Drawing D

Drawing E, a "Carteaadacktoe," was drawn by a fourteen-year-old girl, Tippi, who had an enmeshed, symbiotic relationship to her mother, having been raised as the mother's companion from infancy forward. The NEA drawing indicates the immature quality of this adolescent's personality development. She stated that this was a little animal with a sharp point on top of its head, that runs into trees and knocks leaves down so it has something to eat. Symbolically this depicts Tippi's difficulty in getting her needs met; and despite her enmeshed, "close" relationship, how needful and uncertain she felt about being cared for.

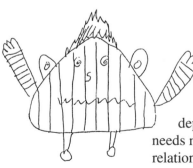

Drawing E

Drawing F

Drawing F by Jeremy, a pre-teen "Gloomy Gus," was produced in response to a request for "a picture of a boy." This drawing shows a small, sad-appearing child with a container area at his stomach. Asked of the meaning, Jeremy stated, "That's where the feelings are...you can put them all in there." Jeremy was a loner, having only one, much younger companion. He spoke often of dying and "getting lost," and the drawing speaks to his felt inadequacy, emptiness and deeply painful emotion.

Drawing G is a self-portrait drawn by an eleven-year-old adoptee, Craig. This young boy had been sexually abused over several years by

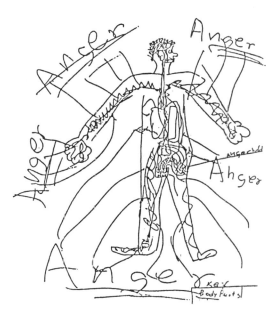

Drawing G

an older "grandpa-like" friend of his aunt and uncle, with whom he lived prior to his adoption. At the time Craig produced this drawing, his adoptive parents brought him to psychotherapy upon discovery that he had forced their two younger children to masturbate. As the drawing shows, Craig is overwhelmingly angry. There are anatomical features depicted with an emphasis on the genital area (which he indicated is a repository for anger) described as a "Jack-in-the-box." Craig was felt to be a "high risk" for sexual perpetration, and when several neighbor children reported sexual molestation by him, he was placed in a residential treatment facility.

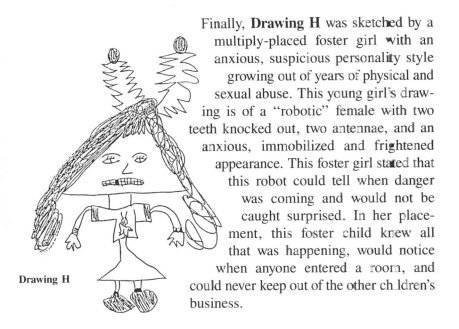
Drawing H

Finally, **Drawing H** was sketched by a multiply-placed foster girl with an anxious, suspicious personality style growing out of years of physical and sexual abuse. This young girl's drawing is of a "robotic" female with two teeth knocked out, two antennae, and an anxious, immobilized and frightened appearance. This foster girl stated that this robot could tell when danger was coming and would not be caught surprised. In her placement, this foster child knew all that was happening, would notice when anyone entered a room, and could never keep out of the other children's business.

Concluding Remarks

In this chapter we have highlighted the characteristics of the maltreated child—the child who is eventually placed in foster or adoptive care. We discussed five prominent types of disturbed children: antisocial, overanxious/insecure, withdrawn/asocial, inadequate/dependent, and mixed type. Each has its own hallmark symptoms, although in reality there can be a great deal of overlap. Importantly, the symptoms shown by disturbed foster and adoptive children stem from their negative view of the world—from their mental blueprint. Drawings presented at the end of this chapter illustrate pictorially and symbolically the inner world of the maltreated child and underscore his cynical sense of the world—and of caregivers in particular. As we will see in the next chapter, the child's negative view of himself and caregivers remains with him long after he is removed from the source of maltreatment. Indeed, in the foster or adoptive home the disturbed child's negative mental blueprint contributes to "reenactment," the recreation of his earlier dysfunctional relationships with new caregivers.

"Only life knowledge produces competence in living. Only the family can teach the most basic knowledge there is: how to live."

Leontyne Young

3 | The Foster or Adoptive Family

T he present chapter looks at the family system in a new way, especially as it appears after placement of disturbed foster or adoptive children. The premise herein is that very unique, yet predictable, patterns emerge in fostering or adopting the disturbed child. Historically, traditional family systems theory has viewed the disturbed child as a symptom of family dysfunction, marital problems and communication difficulties within the family. That is, the child's disturbance acts as a barometer of negative family pressures: as family pressure builds, the child manifests emotional or behavioral problems. Traditional family theory has been immeasurably helpful in understanding, for example, how a biological child with emotional problems may reflect irregularities in his family. However, with foster and adoptive families traditional family theory is not as helpful and in fact, may be misleading and even destructive to the placement. In contrast to the traditional theory, we will discuss a new point of view about how the foster or adoptive child's disturbance creates dysfunction within the home. That is, any dysfunction in the foster or adoptive family may in great part reflect "pressure" (pre-existing emotional disturbance) in the child. In short, this chapter will address what happens when the foster or adoptive family "imports pathology" (in the person of the foster or adoptive child) into its home. We will discuss how the new family becomes the unwitting victim of the child's present disturbance and past exposure to maltreatment.

Traditional Family Systems Theory

"When a family takes on an adoptive or foster child, they often, as it were, 'transplant' a diseased young shoot into their family garden."

Traditional family systems theory emphasizes how an individual's problems relate to larger problems within his family. For example, depression in a child may be seen as reflective of larger family issues, such as maternal depression. Or problems with anger in the child might be symptomatic of unspoken hostility between mother and father or between parent and grandparent. Understanding how marital and communication problems in a family relate to puzzling emotional and behavioral problems in children has added immeasurably to our ability to treat children's difficulties by helping the family.

Ironically, it is the strength of traditional family systems thinking which—applied to adoptive and foster care—is its great weakness. Typically the "power" of family work is that it suggests a larger, "systemic" explanation for problems in the child and removes that child from a harmful, "scapegoat" role. Once seen from the perspective of family, individual, marital and other problems can be dealt with more productively. Unfortunately the traditional approach overlooks or underestimates the flip side—the effect of a dysfunctional individual upon the family as a whole. In the traditional view of the family system, the child is the thermometer which reflects family temperature; as things heat up the mercury rises in the child. In this view the child is a passive measure of the active family process. By contrast, in foster and adoptive families the disturbed child is more thermostat than thermometer. As the family thermostat, the problem child is "set" at a specific temperature; he controls the emotional climate in his new family.

Unfortunately, when looking for causes of the child's disturbance, traditional family theory often erroneously points the finger of blame at the foster or adoptive family. At the same time, the child gets off scot-free—the supposed blameless victim of a malfunctioning foster or adoptive family. But what about the child who is the victimizer rather than the victim? And furthermore, what of the child who was deeply disturbed long before placement with the family?

Central to our work with foster and adoptive families is the notion of "importing pathology." Specifically, by "importing" the child's psychopathology into the home, foster and adoptive families have—

sometimes unsuspectingly—invited into their home the child's pain, upset, paranoia, anxiety and anger. Moreover, the child's view of the world and learned patterns of behavior come along for the ride. While many families have welcomed children in with open arms, they did not count on the severity of the problems which are part of "the package." In effect, when a family takes on an adoptive or foster child, they often, as it were, "transplant" a diseased young shoot into their family garden. The planting, to continue the metaphor, often bears bitter fruit. Further, the whole garden is affected. Eventually family problems—predictable, dramatic and often fatal to the placement—unfold.

The Need for A Revised Family Systems Approach

It is beyond the scope of this book to present a revision of family systems theory. However, it may be helpful to discuss the need for such a revision and what can go wrong when professionals adhere to unchanged, traditional views about family systems without an understanding of the differences inherent in adoption and foster care.

Before discussing the need for revision of traditional notions about family systems, consider this case:

*   *   *   *   *

The Browns, Tom and Tana, were a childless couple who were close to finalizing the adoption of Shayla, age ten. Shayla, a pretty, intelligent young girl, had been in "mortal conflict" with the mother, Tana Brown, since her placement five months earlier. By contrast, Shayla instantly "hit it off" with Tom. When the family sought professional help—at the advice of their adoptive worker—they reported deep marital problems, which included frequent conflicts, disagreements and a brief separation. Tana attributed much of the marital disharmony to Shayla's toxic presence in the home. Tana also viewed Shayla as seductive, manipulative and "fakey" in her relationship to Tom. On the other hand, Tom experienced none of the problem behaviors, power struggles and defiance that his wife reported. He stated that he had been enjoying the time spent with Shayla, and he felt that his wife was exaggerating, overreacting and aloof towards the child.

The mental health therapist completed a brief assessment of the child and adoptive family and recommended individual play therapy for Shayla and family therapy for the adoptive parents. After three months the situation had worsened; despite treatment the adoptive mother gave the ultimatum to her husband: "Either the child goes, or I go." The adoptive father, convinced of his wife's irrationality and frustrated by constant quarrels with her, moved out of the home with the child. The adoptive mother, not surprisingly, felt blamed, guilty, inadequate and misunderstood.

* * * * *

Similar to the case above, many adoptive and foster home parents, especially when inexperienced, quickly find themselves in crisis soon after the placement of a disturbed child. Some parents eventually find their way into the office of a mental health professional. By the time of their initial session, the child's disturbance has transformed the family. The obvious diagnostic temptation for the mental health professional upon meeting the child and family is mistakenly to view the "transformed" —and often dysfunctional family—as the source of the child's problem, thus adding "another nail to the coffin." This focus on foster or adoptive parent problems exonerates the disturbed child, while it "scapegoats" the parents. (In defense of the mental health professional, many foster and adoptive families do appear beleaguered, distressed and downright dysfunctional at this stage of the placement. By the time of their first meeting with the therapist, the couple's marriage is on the ropes, their mental and sometimes physical health is suffering, and they each view the problem in radically different ways. These parents may sharply disagree about parenting approaches, whether the child has problems, and whether the placement should continue. Typically the mother feels that she is the target of anger, passive-aggression and vengeance from the child, while the father enjoys a somewhat idealized relationship to him. In effect, at this stage in placement, they have each experienced a very different child.)

The mental health professional (and often the caseworker, teacher, extended family members and family friends) views the foster or adoptive mother as emotionally reactive, as over-controlling or under-involved, as cold or removed, as hostile or volatile, and as deeply uncommitted or discouraged—based upon how she appears in the initial therapy sessions. Oftentimes mistakenly, the professional perceives the mother's current functioning (or should we say, "dysfunctioning") as an indication of on-going, long-standing personal/emotional problems which have interfered with the placed child's ability to incorporate into the family and to properly bond with her.

Professionals characteristically take sides with the father and child— with the father who appears more rational, available and stable, and with the child who seems to be the victim of the mother's rejection and emotional problems.

Although it is most commonly the mother who is "incriminated" by the mental health professional, caseworker and others, sometimes the child's disturbance is blamed on the father, both parents or the family as a whole. Again, at least in the case of the mental health professional, it is often assumptions from traditional family systems theory which misguide him/her to suppose that it is the off-kilter family dynamic which underlies the foster (or adoptive) child's difficulty with incorporating into the family. Rarely do professionals recognize adequately the child's pathology and its damaging effect on the foster/adoptive family.

"Rarely do professionals recognize adequately the child's pathology and its damaging effect on the foster/adoptive family."

Some Notions About Foster and Adoptive Family Systems

We will be discussing in the next sections several notions about foster and adoptive families, which differ substantially from traditional theories about disturbed children and dysfunctional families. First, of primary importance in understanding what can happen to foster and adoptive families, is an appreciation of what we call the "reverse effect," the disturbed child's impact on the family. Secondly, we will discuss the phenomenon of "splitting," which explains why individual family members and others experience such different sides to the disturbed child. Thirdly, we will address the stages which are "typical" for the adoptive or foster family to pass through—especially if they are unprepared and inexperienced—with the placement of the disturbed child. Fourth, we will summarize the child's historic family relationships, which have often been abusive, neglectful, and/or exploitive. These historic relationships set the stage for unhealthy, conflict-ridden relationships in the foster or adoptive home. Lastly, we will discuss the child's negative mental blueprint (his expectations and prejudices about parents, intimacy and family life) and the process of "reenactment," the child's stubborn tendency to re-live old, destructive parent-child relationships in the foster or adoptive home.

Reverse Effect

By now it must be clear to the reader that the placed child is not a passive player in the foster or adoptive home. Indeed, the child can consciously or unconsciously influence relationships within the home and the relative stability or instability of the placement. Truly, where the child's disturbance is intransigent, he may evoke debilitating problems in family members. When the child negatively influences the family, a "reverse effect" has occurred (see Illustration 3.1). The direction of influence is not from the top down—from the parents to the child. Rather, it is from the bottom up — child to parent. (Many foster and adoptive parents have mentioned in frustration, "The child is definitely on top

Illustration 3.1 The Reverse Effect

in this family!") The reverse effect may be related to the child's negative mental blueprint, tendency to split (see next section), and to his penchant for reenactment (see ahead). However, in some cases so-called reverse effects might also be the result of medical/psychiatric/neurological problems, as seen next:

* * * * *

The foster mother stated with a note of defeat that she and her husband had tried everything they could to control Randy's misbehavior but were, in her words, "losing the battle." (The foster mother appeared depressed and the foster father complained of a stomach ulcer and appeared somewhat agitated and "jumpy.") A battle royal had developed in the foster home, permeating every aspect of life with the child. Randy, age 10, resisted and opposed every adult suggestion, request and direction. When asked to finish his plate at the supper table, Randy spat onto his plate and smeared it around on the table cloth. In addition, Randy had made several suicide attempts, once taking a large quantity of aspirin and on another occasion drinking some cleaning fluid. Moreover, Randy often seemed "out of it," "spacey" and according to the foster father, "marching to the beat of a different drummer." A psychiatric and neurological evaluation suggested a seizure disorder, which was later confirmed by abnormal EEG findings. Prescribed an anti-convulsant medication (to prevent seizures), Randy would resist taking the medication and/or pretend to swallow his pill only to spit it out later. Blood tests revealed that the boy had successfully kept the medication out of his system. Further, Randy quickly learned how to precipitate seizures when he wanted to. The caseworker sought out openings in institutional settings, since Randy's behavior continued to deteriorate. Fortunately, the foster parents were instructed by the neurologist in ways to insure that Randy was taking his medication. After two weeks of actually swallowing his pills, Randy made a dramatic improvement. The foster father portrayed him as "a different kid altogether...he is much more 'with it' and doesn't argue over every small point." Randy's eyes sparkled and he seemed to understand and comply with requests from the foster mother. The transformation made this boy manageable in the foster family situation. He was no longer a suicide risk; he related with improved eye contact; and, in general, he was now a positive, up-beat sort of kid.

* * * * *

In some instances, it is not merely the child's exposure to abuse, neglect and exploitation which has rendered him so disturbed. Some foster and adoptive children have medical/neurological/psychiatric problems which make them almost totally untreatable in the family environment. In Randy's case, he had both a history of maltreatment and an underlying neurological problem (the seizure disorder). The combination was almost fatal to the placement. His disturbance had nearly undermined the placement and had had a "reverse effect" on the foster parents. By their appearance during the initial meetings with the mental health professional, the foster parents could have been mistaken as the source of the child's problems. The oppositional behavior might have been seen as the child's attempt to engage a depressed and withdrawing foster mother, for instance.

(And with the foster father in such a high state of anxiety and "jumpiness," what child wouldn't be anxious at the dinner table? That is, maybe the father's stomach problems and the child's spitting at the dinner table were correlated!) As a matter of fact, the behaviors of the child and parents were interrelated. However, it was the child's "imported pathology" which was taking its toll on an otherwise normal pair of foster parents. The child's unlimited power struggling and repulsive table behavior were exhausting the foster mother and making the foster father "sick to his stomach"—the reverse effect.

In summary, the reverse effect is a very common occurrence in foster and adoptive families. The child's very powerful impact—often negative—on the host family is typical and yet often overlooked by helping professionals. A disturbed child with fetal alcohol syndrome, attention deficit hyperactivity disorder, psychotic features, or an affective (mood) disorder can easily upset the equilibrium of an otherwise stable family. When this child has also experienced abuse, neglect, and/or exploitation, the probability of severe negative impact increases.

The Phenomenon of Splitting

Why do foster (or adoptive) mothers and fathers see their children so differently from one another? For that matter, why are professionals' perceptions of the child so different from that of the mother? Similarly, why do in-laws, other relatives, neighbors and friends of the family experience the disturbed foster/adoptive child so differently from the mother? Answers to these questions are found in an understanding of "splitting."

A satirist once said, "There are two kinds of people in the world: those who divide the world into two kinds of people and those who don't." Disturbed children often live in a black-and-white world; they see only two kinds of people in the world: good and bad. "Splitting" is the psychological phenomenon—an inner defense—which explains why troubled foster and adoptive children think in such all-or-nothing terms. Some classic examples of splitting are:

• The child views himself alternately as all-wonderful or as totally worthless.

• The child idealizes the foster or adoptive father and devalues the mother.

• The child views his teacher or caseworker positively for awhile, then when he feels aggrieved or wronged, he suddenly rejects totally.

• The child perceives maltreating biological parents as sainted and the foster or adoptive parents as devilish.

Splitting is a psychological defense inherent in all humans. It is only pathological when the categorization is rigid, unbending and patently false. Pathological splitting occurs when a child has failed to integrate the good and bad feelings which arise towards his first caregivers. This failure to see caregivers in shades of gray often derives from situations in which the child is precluded from expressing angry feelings towards his caregivers. In cases of abuse, neglect and exploitation, the child may be prevented from expressing mounting anger and frustration. Threats to the child of abuse, rejection and abandonment by the parent force him to deny and suppress any angry feelings towards that parent. The anger is said to be "split off." This explains why abused children so desperately and completely elevate their maltreating parents and seem totally unaware of the justifiable anger and frustration with them. But where do the "split off" feelings go? These feelings emerge in other ways and often attach to other individuals, to the foster or adoptive parents or to the child himself, as in the following case example:

* * * * *

Garth, a nine-year-old foster boy, was suicidal and self-destructive after each visit with his birth mother. Before these visits Garth would work himself into an ecstatic lather. However, his ecstacy was soon followed by agony. Garth excitedly bragged to the other foster children about pending visits, the promised gifts he was going to receive from his mother, and how wonderful his mother was to him. When his mother arrived for the visit—oftentimes late—she became loud, obnoxious and self-absorbed. While Garth acted like a "puppy dog" around her, pathetically he was "barking up the wrong tree." His mother seemed oblivious to Garth and his needs. When he attempted, for example, to tell her of his recent accomplishments in math, his mother reminisced about how well she had done in math as a child, discounting Garth's need for recognition. Throughout visits his mother typically dismissed what Garth told her or showed open displeasure at his normal childhood exuberance. For instance, during one visit in the park, Garth strayed briefly from his mother's side and met up with some younger children on a merry-go-round. Rushing to his mother excitedly, he exclaimed, "Mom, Mom...they like me and want to play with me!" In response, his mother gave Garth a look that could kill. She expected total homage from him during visits and punished him with a disdainful, emasculating glance which communicated, "How could you treat me so poorly?" For all intents and purposes, the visit in the park had ended at that very moment. Though Garth attempted frantically to win his mother's acceptance, he never succeeded. He would sit at her side and chat nervously in a desperate attempt to pacify her. Next, he resorted to asking inane questions to engage her; but it was futile. A cold chill had settled across his mother's now motionless face. She refused even to talk, and in stony silence they returned to the foster home.

That evening Garth bashed his head deliberately into a door jamb, leaving a goose egg on his forehead; he also self-mutilated—carving on his arms with a paper clip until he drew blood; and he dropped a weight set on his toe "accidentally." The foster father eventually had to restrain Garth physically. Any questions from the foster parents about the visit or his mother were met with rageful defensiveness.

* * * * *

In the case illustration, Garth, an insecure, overanxious child around his biological mother, split off anger towards her and directed it towards himself and others in the foster home. His foster mother reported that Garth, after visits, acted like a "blind snake, striking out at anything warm." While Garth experienced nothing but frustration of his needs with his biological mother, he denied, supressed and repressed any minute negative emotion towards her. He had learned early in his relationship to her that such negative emotion was punished unmercifully. Directing anger towards himself and the foster parents provided a safer outlet.

The topic of splitting ties into our earlier discussion of the "mental blueprint." The child, in cases like Garth, is consciously aware of only the positive feelings towards his birth mother. Indeed, she is placed upon a pedestal. Yet the internalized mental blueprint about mothers is negative, based upon the years of neglect of his needs. There is a wide disparity between what Garth has experienced of his mother and what he lets himself feel about her. Only outside the relationship with her and away from her presence can Garth express what he truly feels about mothers: that they are harsh, rejecting, self-absorbed and unavailable.

The child who has been separated from or lost past mother figures (or, one who has been abused, neglected or exploited by mothers) brings a combination of unmet and unrecognized needs and smoldering anger at the primary caregiver (usually the mother) into the foster-adoptive home. In a sense the child sees any "new" mother as the one who hurt, rejected and abandoned him in the past. His behavior towards her can be abusive, rejecting, clinging and overanxious. Or, he can feel ambivalent about the new mother, displaying a confusing array of love-hate, push-pull reactions towards her. Some perplexed foster/adoptive mothers have characterized the child as "hanging on with one hand and hitting with the other." In the process, the surrogate mother becomes the undeserving "victim" of the child's past. In any case, the relationship to the foster or adoptive mother is often quite intense and simultaneously negative or ambivalent.

Disturbed foster and adoptive children often develop a fundamentally different—more idealized—relationship to the father figure in a "new" home. The intensity of the anger or ambivalence, as seen in our clinical experience, towards foster and adoptive fathers is much more diluted, if present at all. We have two theories about this difference: the first concerns the fact that father figures have often not been primary caregivers to the child. Moreover, issues surrounding attachment, separation, abandonment and rejection may be less serious relative to the father. The child with unresolved grief for his lost mother or mothers is reluctant to trust a new mother and typically harbors many more feelings of rage towards her over perceived abandonment. By the same token, the child who has only had peripheral involvement with past father figures, has less distrust of future father figures and stores less resentment towards them. Admittedly, some past father-figures have been abusive, harsh and rejecting; thus, a later response by the child to his foster/adoptive father is one of fear, avoidance and muted anger. Our second theory is that foster and adoptive mothers are not only the primary caregivers but are also the chief disciplinarians in the home. Nitty-gritty limit-setting, punishment, and child guidance places these mothers in hand-to-hand combat with disturbed children. The disciplinarian role invites feelings and expressions of anger from the child.

Common Stages in Placement

Even well-functioning, reasonably balanced families begin to change for the worse when they are under the prolonged stress of living with the disturbed foster/adoptive child. Families that are truly "sub-clinical" in their adjustment—those who are essentially normal, having raised prior healthy children, maintained stable employment, and built satisfying, intact marital/family lives—can appear "clinical" or dysfunctional under the unique stress of "imported" problems.

Once problems are imported into the home, the family passes through certain stages (see Illustration 3.2). Commonly the family begins the placement with an optimistic—if mildly apprehensive—view about their desire and ability to help the disturbed child. This is the stage of "pre-placement fantasy." A prime example of this occurs in situations where a potential adoptive family hears about, reads about or views an adoptable child on television or video tape. The attraction to the child may be almost "chemical." This reaction is not unlike what happens following the birth of a child, when the biological parents become enamored of the little wrinkled being in the delivery room. During the pre-placement fantasy, the parents cannot wait to get started in their role as caregivers. Their enthusiasm and unflagging optimism may also be accompanied by a tendency to minimize the child's problems—especially true in cases wherein the foster or adoptive family has never raised a disturbed child before—and to believe that "love is enough" to help him. Soon after the placement, the adoptive family may "take the baby and run," so to speak. That is, in their eagerness to get started in parenting, they may prematurely try to avoid, flee and free themselves from the adoptive agency, caseworkers and other professionals. Unfortunately this may divorce them from potential sources of help and advice when problems begin to emerge. All too often adoptive families do not re-connect with helping professionals until it's almost too late—once they have "had it" with the disturbed child.

After the child is placed, the optimistic family fantasy is often initially reinforced during the "honeymoon stage." "Honeymooning" can last from a matter of hours to several weeks or months. During this stage the disturbed child suspends temporarily his misbehavior, curtails outlandish acting-out, and in effect lulls the family into a false sense of complacency. (As you may know, many disturbed children make a good "first impression." Only later does their tendency to sabotage intimacy and to recreate negative relationships from the past begin to emerge.)

The third stage, which we call "mother's discovery," consists of a common phenomenon in foster and adoptive placements. Typically, the mothers in such placements are the first to recognize the child's underlying and pervasive disturbance. Mothers, as the primary caregivers in most families, become targets for the child's bottomless neediness, teeming anger and confusing ambivalence.

In stage four, the "marital split," we note a growing rift between the foster or adoptive couple. By this stage couples have begun to see and to interact with the child in very different ways. The foster/adoptive father, in his oft-times role of "playmate" or of evening-and-weekend-dad, is a more peripheral, less significant figure to the disturbed child. Importantly, the father is less involved in the "nitty-gritty" parental job of disciplining the children. By contrast the mother becomes an exceedingly threatening, albeit coveted, figure to the child. To the disturbed child, she is the parent who abused, neglected, rejected and exploited him in the past; he behaves accordingly. Thus, she inherits the role of all past maltreating mothers. At the same time, the foster or adoptive father enjoys a rather uncomplicated, conflict-free relationship to the disturbed child, who may place this father-figure on a pedestal. The upshot of all this is that each parent knows and experiences a different child. Unless the differences between the couple are resolved and the child's damaging impact recognized by both parents, the placement will be jeopardized. Without immediate outside intervention and assistance, the entire family situation may devolve to the final stage, "placement disruption," with a devastating impact on the marriage.

Illustration 3.2 Common Stages In Placement

Pre-placement Fantasy

The "Honeymoon"

Mother's Discovery

The Marital Split

Placement Disruption

Sub-clinical Levels of Pathology

We might point out here that very few marriages and individuals are without imperfection, dysfunction and an "Achilles' Heel." In our work with families, we have come to think of individuals as having "sub-clinical" (non-interferring, insignificant) levels of emotional problems which only come to the surface under adverse, stressful conditions. Foster and adoptive parents' "sub-clinical" emotional issues become "clinical" after the disturbed child has added undue stress to the marriage and family. (To reiterate, the very disturbed child recreates the past in the present family; that is, he transfers his old pattern of behaving into the present situation, to which the unwitting adoptive (or foster) family may fall prey, as we see in the next case):

* * * * *

The Monors, Robert and JoAnn, prospective adoptive parents of two boys, were having second thoughts as the finalization date approached. The boys, Mark and Mike (siblings, age 4 and 8 respectively), had a host of problems, behavioral and emotional. Exceedingly neglected as infants and toddlers, Mark and Mike had been forced to raise themselves—modern "feral" children. They were hyperactive, chaotic and disruptive in eight foster homes. Mark and Mike were freed for adoption while they were living at the Jones' Group Home. The welfare department approached Robert and JoAnn Monors, who had been on a waiting list for a baby or toddler, preferrably male. They convinced the Monors to take Mike and Mark as a "packaged deal." Without any "honeymoon" stage behavior problems erupted. Within two months the placement was in deep jeopardy, the Monors' marriage was strained, and Mrs. Monors in particular looked quite harried and angry. Her mother-in-law felt that the boys were "lovely children" who needed more "TLC." Mr. Monors sided with his mother, since he saw the boys as pleasant and playful in the evenings when he returned from work. He had a difficult time imagining that they were as much trouble as his wife found them to be during the day. The rift between Mr. and Mrs. Monors was widened inadvertantly by the children's psychotherapist, who never conferred with the Monors about how things were going in placement. This therapist viewed the boys as "loveable and highly adoptable," and concluded that Mrs. Monors was an emotionally unavailable "refrigerator mother."

* * * * *

The above case provides a classic scenario of potential adoption disruption. In this case, a home study completed before the placement found Mr. and Mrs. Monors to be intelligent, emotionally available, stable, every-day people, perfect for adopting a "waiting child—or two." The Monors' marriage was seen as solid, trusting and based on similar, consonant values; they were "good stock, salt-of-the-earth, and All-American." The questions arise: Did the home study miss the mark? Was there hidden pathology which the adoption agency failed to uncover? Did the family have insidious, unhealthy reasons for wanting to adopt in the first place? The answer to all of these questions is flatly "no." The key to determining what went wrong in this family lies in understanding the destructive impact of an emotionally disturbed child on the adoptive or foster family. That impact stems from the child's "mental blueprint" of the world—his perceptions of and expectations about what mothers, fathers, and families are all about.

Pre-exisiting, Bona Fide Psychopathology in the Foster/Adoptive Family

Some foster and adoptive parents have been beset by emotional troubles, marital strife, and full-blown psychiatric disorders prior to the placement of the disturbed child. Because of such pre-existing problems, these parents find the task of raising and caring for disturbed children especially taxing. In addition, unresolved or debilitating disorders may erode their ability to help the children in their care. In the worst case scenario, a serious disturbance in the foster or adoptive parent can contribute to further damage to the already "injured" child, as seen next.

* * * * *

As an upper-class married couple from a prosperous suburb, Mr. and Mrs. Erickson had few problems obtaining approval for adoption from a church-affiliated agency. Unfortunately, the cursory home-study disregarded Mrs. Erickson's subtle but significant mental health difficulties and her truly lacklustre motivation to adopt. In addition, the study downplayed the signs of Mr. Erickson's "workaholism." Beneath the social correctness, Mrs. Erickson was a lonely, chronically unhappy, childless woman in her mid-thirties, who had never recovered from the loss of her own mother. She felt no strong desire to adopt, but had complied with her husband's request to have a son. To the adoption agency, and to those who knew this family socially, the adoption of Evan, a mildly troubled thirteen-year-old boy, had seemed quite appropriate, since the couple had been sponsors of the parish Young Christian's Assembly for a number of years. However, the adoption floundered, and

Evan seemed anxious and unsettled after six months with the Erickson's. He additionally began to withdraw and isolate himself in his room. Various professionals hypothesized that it was Evan's disturbance that was "rearing its ugly head." They seemed to overlook Mrs. Erickson's lack of true interest in the adoption from the very start. The agency was almost as surprised as Mr. Erickson when his wife—one day before the adoption was to be finalized—announced abruptly her desire to leave "an intolerable marriage."

* * * * *

Fortunately, occurrences like that described above are rare; however, it is true that some foster and adoptive parents are unfit to care for the disturbed child—or perhaps any children. Their rigidity, fragility, emotional dysfunctions, and sordid motives are sometimes totally overlooked during evaluations prior to the placement of a child in their home. The couple whose bankrupt marriage seeks a child to lend life to their defunct union, or the depressed parent who uses foster or adoptive children to meet his/her needs—these are situations in which "bona fide" pathology exists. In such instances the child's behavioral problems may truly reflect the pathology of the foster or adoptive couple.

Dysfunction in the Child's Family of Origin

The maltreated child's mental blueprint obviously is shaped by his past experience with caregivers and family life. Commonly, the severely disturbed foster or adoptive child comes from one of three egregiously dysfunctional family types: abusive, neglectful or exploitive. We want to note here that these three types can show a great deal of overlap. That is, some families can exploit and neglect, abuse and exploit, and so on. However, seriously dysfunctional families typically have dominant characteristics which allow them to be classified into one of three categories.

The Abusive Type

The "abusive" type of dysfunctional family (see Table 3.1) is characterized by episodes of explosive parental anger; inappropriately harsh discipline; scapegoating of an easily targeted child; unrealistically high expectations for the child; extreme intolerance for individuality; excessive demand for compliance; vacillation between over-strictness and permissiveness; and idealization and devaluation of the child, as seen in the following case:

* * * * *

In the Graves family, dangerous abuse ran rampant. Of the four children Clarence, age six, was clearly the most frequent target for physical abuse by his father, a brooding man with a ballistic temper. Clarence received no help or protection from his passive-submissive mother. The root of the father's deep hostility towards Clarence was the fact that the boy had been conceived during an extramarital affair by his wife—her secret revenge for her husband's many drunken infidelities.

Clarence, a kindergartner, came to the attention of school personnel because of his bossy, intimidating and malicious behavior towards other children on the playground. (Clarence knocked one boy unconscious in a rock-throwing incident. He argued without any sign of remorse that the boy "had it coming.") In the classroom Clarence was encopretic, soiling his pants several times each school day. In an interview with the school psychologist, Clarence revealed that he was terrified of his father who spanked him mercilessly for minor behavior problems and who battered his mother.

The social worker's visit to the home found that Mr. Graves held iron-fisted control of his wife and children. Even when sober Mr. Graves was an unrelenting, unbending tyrant in the house. Though no one completely escaped the abuse, Clarence took the brunt of it. (Clarence stood as a flesh-and-blood reminder to both parents of Mrs. Graves' one, feeble attempt at standing up to her dictatorial husband.) To add to the problem, Mrs. Graves in her passivity towards all males—young and old alike— was submissive to Clarence when her husband was not at home. By contrast to her husband's inhuman control over his son, Mrs. Graves was a "Rodney Dangerfield" mother-figure, who "got no respect" from Clarence or from her other children.

* * * * *

"Family life" in homes like the Graves conditions the abused child to expect the unexpected, to be wary of those whom he should trust the most. Children like Clarence are shaped to comply and submit blindly, all the while they must keep their eyes wide open. Any expression of normal independence of thought, disagreement with, or frustration towards the abusive parent is expunged by severe punishments or threats. Often the only ventilation of mounting anger occurs in the presence of "safe" adults or children; in this case Clarence "took it out on" his mother and on children on the playground. Abused children must often displace the anger originating elsewhere onto safer targets such as the school, younger children and the foster or adoptive family. Ironically, the abusive family often reports a lack of acting-out, aggression or anger by the child in their home. In essence, when abusive parents report that they have no problems with the child at home, it is an accurate portrayal—but what is left out is a recognition of the child's fear and anger, an admission of their own abusiveness, and an understanding of the child's denial and suppression of his feelings in the home.

TABLE 3.1 Characteristics of the Abusive Family

- Episodes of explosive parental anger.
- Inappropriately harsh discipline.
- Scapegoating of an easily-targeted child.
- Unrealistically high expectations for the child.
- Extreme intolerance for individuality.
- Excessive demand for compliance.
- Vacillating between over-strictness and permissiveness.
- Idealization and devaluation of the child.

The Neglectful Type

Neglectful families—possibly the most dysfunctional of all families and those who may leave the deepest "invisible scars" on the child—fail to provide for the child's needs for medical care, food and shelter, education, parental supervision and stimulation. These are the families who are isolated and lonely and without support systems. They are marked by instability, loose bonds and poverty. (This is not to say that wealthy or middle class families are incapable of neglecting their children. However, the additional weight of financial destitution crushes hope, vitality and capacity to parent, producing a state of "apathy-futility.") Table 3.2 lists the characteristics of neglectful families, some of which are described in the following case study:

* * * * *

The Donner family had a long history of contacts with child protection agencies in several states due to allegations of neglect of the children. Mr. and Mrs. Donner had recently moved to town in a car that gave out just as they entered the city limits. Both unemployed and recently evicted from their mobile home, they were low-functioning intellectually and had each dropped out of school special education programs in their mid-teens. Mr. and Mrs. Donner had six ragamuffin children who ranged in age from six months to twelve years. The older children attended school in soiled, urine-soaked clothing. They were generally unkempt, unwashed and smelly. Other students made fun of them and ostracized them. The youngest child, an unsmiling baby with a dull look in her eyes, sat in the crib nearly all day without crying. This baby had been diagnosed as understimulated and a "failure to thrive." She was not brought in for follow-up doctor visits to monitor her growth. The most recent neglect report to be filed against the family occurred when the oldest boy, age twelve, had been found wandering alone on a downtown street at midnight.

When the child protection worker made her first home visit, she found the residence to be unheated and without water and phone. There were trash and broken glass piled high in the yard, leaving no room for the children to play safely. Inside, the trailer was crowded and non-hygienic. There were dirty dishes stacked high on every horizontal surface in the kitchen; and there were animal feces smeared into the carpet. A loaded gun lay on a coffee table. The television screen provided the only light in the house, as the curtains were drawn in every room. Surprisingly, the Donners did not appear noticeably upset about the caseworker's visit.

*   *   *   *   *

Neglectful families similar to the Donners are identified in both urban and rural settings all across the United States. These families are marked by apathy and futility—a condition light years beyond clinical depression. The tragic lives of neglectful parents beget more tragic lives in their offspring. Family life for these children provides little in the way of protection, warmth, understanding, sensitivity and stimulation. While the family may live in close quarters, there is very little else which might be called "close" about family life.

TABLE 3.2 Characteristics of the Neglectful Family

- Poor negotiation among family members.
- Isolation within the family.
- Resistance to accepting responsibility.
- Stunted range of emotional expression.
- Lack of empathy.
- Lack of appropriate supervision and monitoring of the children.

The Exploitive Type

The exploitive family (see Table 3.3), is the third major dysfunctional family type. Characteristically, exploitive families are marked by symbiosis; by periods of "intermittent enmeshment" with a needy parent; by blurred boundaries (sometimes sexual) between parent and child; by role reversals; and by a global failure to recognize the child's needs as separate and distinct from their own. (Of course, some exploitive families are "sexually exploitive" as well. We refer to "exploitive" as a pervasive condition, only sometimes including sexual victimization of the child.) Exploited youngsters are treated as objects by the parents and become servants to their needs, as seen in the next case illustration:

*   *   *   *   *

The Tatum family consisted of Mrs. Tatum, a single, unstable mother and her only child, Robert. Mrs. Tatum was an attractive but emotionally desperate woman who could not be without a man. She had an inordinate number of fleeting relationships with lovers over the ten years of Robert's life. Between lovers Mrs. Tatum—in her unfathomable loneliness—turned to Robert for companionship and comfort. At those "in-between" times, Robert was "Momma's little man." He was invited to sleep with his mother, who had never overcome her childish fears of the dark. During these times the relationship between Mrs. Tatum and Robert grew unnaturally strong, given the intensity of their "enmeshment." They did everything and went everywhere together—with Robert often "excused" from school to stay with his mother. However, just as soon as Mrs. Tatum attracted another adult male lover, Robert was relegated to his bedroom again, and the "plug was pulled" on the all-too-cozy mother-son relationship. Over time, the on-again-off-again nature of their relationship rendered Robert anxious and angry. He seemed perpetually insecure and clingy; when "on the outs" with his mother, he was rage-filled and vengeful. As he grew older, Robert's angry acting-out increased, and he confronted his mother's latest lover with a baseball bat. In the scuffle which followed, Robert was bruised. After this incident, Mrs. Tatum, fearing the potential loss of her "new man" and frightened of impending loneliness, resorted to a voluntary placement of Robert in foster care.

*   *   *   *   *

In exploitive families the child or children often become remarkably overanxious/insecure, although they can also have an antisocial appearance as well. The nature of their connection to caregivers is highly ambivalent as they are desperately needy of interactions but conditioned to expect periodic abandonment. Ultimately they do not view their needs as being met by the parent figure. Indeed, they—beneath it all—feel enraged at the lack of attention to their real needs. At the same time, they are often very used to dealing with the adult world and seem at least superficially comfortable in the adult arena. They have been trained often to take on a "pseudo-adult" relationship, one in which they take care of the needy, child-like parent figure(s) around them. In a twisted way they vicariously experience care through their "caregiving." However, their negative expectations about inevitable adult rejection, along with their learned role of caregiver, interfere with being a child. In foster or adoptive care these children are loathe to surrender their role of "parentified" child and may resist efforts from caring adults to parent them properly.

TABLE 3.3 Characteristics of the Exploitive Family

- The child is allowed, even encouraged, to take on a parental role.
- The parents expect attention and affection from the child.
- There are blurred boundaries (sometimes sexual) between parent and child.
- The parents do not encourage independence, curiosity or exploration.
- There is a global failure by the parents to recognize the child's needs as separate and distinct from their own.

How the Maltreated Child "Pictures" the Family

The ultimate impact of a seriously dysfunctional family upon the child is a distortion of and injury to his understanding of himself and others—his mental blueprint. As mentioned in Chapter Two, that blueprint manifests itself in the child's behavior, symptoms, verbalizations, symbolic play, relationships, and in his artistic productions. Here we will present and discuss various drawings sketched by disturbed foster and adoptive children. These drawings depict families or select members of families. Along with corroborating information about the child's history, behavior in foster or adoptive placement, and verbalizations about significant others, drawings elucidate how the child views his world, his family and caregivers.

Drawing A, by an eight-year-old adopted boy, Gary, is of himself and his birth mother. Even after he had been in placement for two years, Gary remained distant and wary of the adoptive mother and father. When asked to draw a picture of his biological mother, he crafted this depiction. The drawing portrays the boy as a toddler, with tears streaming down his face. When questioned about the absence of tears from his right eye, Gary asserted, "My

Drawing A

mom did not want me to cry to her... 'Don't let me see you cry.'" In effect, Gary was hiding his feelings from his mother. Splotches between his legs are feces and blood stains, Gary having just been sodomized by his mother's sadistic boyfriend. As you can see, the toddler is held at arm's length by his mother who is—except for her outstretched limbs—off the page. The distance between mother and child along with the absence of the mother from the picture convey loss, lack of nurturance and rejection. Ultimately, Gary was abandoned by his birth mother, who left him to run off with the sexually abusing boyfriend.

In **Drawing B,** a ten-year-old foster boy was asked to draw a picture of his family doing something together. (He was not told which family to draw—his birth or foster family.) He instantly sketched a drawing of his murderously angry stepfather brandishing a knife. As you can see in the drawing, part of the boy's face has been hacked away. In questioning him we found no evidence that he had ever been assaulted physically by the stepfather with a knife or other weapon. Indeed, the "weapons" which the stepfather used against him were his cruel, mentally abusive comments and occasional humiliating physical discipline, during which the stepfather forced the boy to strip naked in front of the family to accept his

Drawing B

spankings.

The next drawing (**Drawing C**) was a disturbed adopted girl's depiction of her birth family. In this sketch the father and mother stand arm in arm, while the children (represented by the encircled five dots) huddle together. This girl had initially drawn only four dots; when asked what the four dots were, she stated, "Oh, I left myself out." She then proceeded to draw a fifth dot. The significance of this drawing lies in the children as dots.

Drawing C

Without knowing the history in this case, it would be a challenge to explain the derivation of the "dot children." However, we knew of the massive neglect and history of abandonment in this family of origin. As you might expect, children in the "dot family" were unimportant to the parents who frequently left them alone and unsupervised.

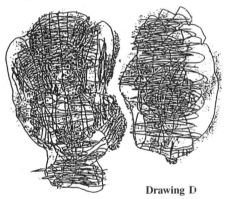

Drawing D

Drawing D is unusual and difficult to decipher. It was drawn by a troubled, frightened seven-year-old boy who had recently been placed after his mother, a single parent, had committed suicide. This boy—the only child of an invalided, isolated and chronically depressed woman—had according to relatives, lived in a symbiotic world with her.

Before her death, this woman had kept him as her constant companion. (He had never been left with a babysitter or with a relative. The child, in fact, had not learned to walk until he was three years of age, his mother carrying him on a hip until he became too heavy for her.) After the mother's suicide the boy was placed in a foster home, as all his relatives lived out of state. When asked to draw a picture of his family, he drew a stranger in a chair (on the left) with a tornado in the background (on the right). As you can see, family for this boy was devoid of anyone familiar; the tornado and the overall frenetic scribbling of the drawing convey a sense of approaching danger and a state of high anxiety.

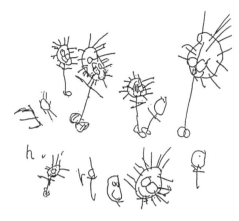

The primitive quality of **Drawing E** is the most noteworthy aspect to the next family picture. The artist, a withdrawn, scattered six-year-old adopted boy, reveals difficulties with fine motor (hand-eye) development, along with a hazy, non-differentiating view of his family. Even though this boy had lived in this family for over half of his life,

Drawing E

he remained a "man without a country." When asked about the individuals he had drawn, this child could not identify who was in the picture. He said, "This big guy is me...no, it is Stevie (a sibling)...or maybe Bob (the adoptive father)...it don't (sic) matter to me." His verbal descriptions of the other figures on the page were as non-committal and shifting. In short, this picture suggests how vaguely this boy viewed his adoptive family, whose members were but interchangeable figures. Sadly, the adoptive parents reported with some sense of hopelessness, "He has never attached to us...to this day I believe he could leave our home tomorrow and not look back."

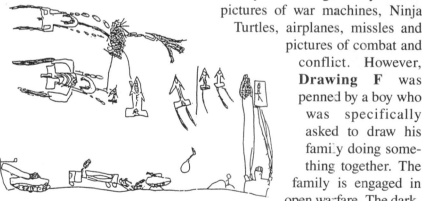

Commonly school-aged boys draw pictures of war machines, Ninja Turtles, airplanes, missles and pictures of combat and conflict. However, **Drawing F** was penned by a boy who was specifically asked to draw his family doing something together. The family is engaged in open warfare. The dark, colored-in oval is this boy's mother. The numerous

Drawing F

missles and warplanes are directing their fire power towards her. The father figure is the tiny stick figure on the lower right of the picture.

He, though hiding behind a small hill, will soon be blown to bits by a bomb dropped on him by his wife. The boy who drew this picture had a great deal of anger at mother figures, as you might surmise, and at the time this picture was drawn, he had "blown out of" his third foster home in as many months. The tiny stick figure in the rectangular box is the boy himself dropping to the ground. He explained that the box is a protective shield which deflects the poison rays shot at him from below.

Drawing G

Drawing G is the handiwork of a disturbed foster girl who had lived with a very unstable and eccentric mother. This girl, age ten, captured well the disapproving, suspicious glance which her birth mother gave her before meting out punishment. What came out during the evaluation of this mother and her daughter was the complete, unquestioning obedience which the mother demanded along with an intolerance of the child's need for independence.

Drawing H, sketched by Daniella, a nine-year-old foster girl, portrays herself naked and captured in a bottle. The drawing depicts her extraordinarily sexualized view of herself, her use as a sexual object, and her "containment"—her inability to escape her abuse. Daniella spontaneously said, "I don't like myself...She looks really sad." This child had been the victim of extreme emotional neglect and sexual abuse by her sole parent, her birth father, who was later convicted of selling pictures of Daniella engaged in sexual acts.

Drawing H

Drawing I

Finally, **Drawing I** was sketched by an eight-year-old girl awaiting adoption. Asked to draw a picture of herself in her birth family, she drew a child surrounded by an aura and halo. The smaller figure in the drawing is the child leaving her body. She described the drawing this way, "This girl is inside here. When she has to leave, she just flies out of her body and goes away... She is good." This child's history indicated she had been sexually victimized by a cavalcade of her mother's boyfriends from a very young age. The horrendous victimization had resulted in severe medical problems. (This sketch suggests that this girl had resorted to "dissociation" during sexual attacks. That is, she escaped in the only way she could—by "leaving her body." Later in foster placement, therapists were concerned about a developing "multiple personality disorder.")

Reenactment

Given their checkered pasts, is it any wonder that maltreated children show such psychopathology in adoptive and foster families? These unfortunate children take into placement a history of family relatedness (or "non-relatedness") which poorly prepares them for incorporation into a home which provides care, warmth, protection, communication, understanding and input. The child's view of caregivers and family life and his learned patterns from his past strongly influence how he acts in his present (foster or adoptive) placement. As seen in the drawings above, the child's view of the world is truly jaundiced and cynical.

Over time the disturbed child's impact on the foster or adoptive family often results in the "new family" resembling the past, maltreating family. That is, the foster or adoptive family may find itself negotiating less and becoming more dictatorial; they may find themselves feeling abusive impulses; they may discover that the youngster has attempted to place them in a child role, while clutching to his habitual role as "pseudo adult;" they may find themselves increasingly estranged and distant from each other; communication between spouses may grow more strained and less clear; and blaming others (agencies, the school system or one's mate) becomes more the family norm. In fact, after the placement of a very troubled, formerly maltreated child, the foster or adoptive family seems to be much more pathological and develops a sense of apathy and futility. We feel that this derives from the stress of taking on a disturbed child and from the deleterious impact of the child's mental blueprint on the family. Specifically, the child reenacts earlier mental and behavioral patterns in placement, and the host family begins to transform into the child's "picture of family." Hence, foster/adoptive families may appear very disturbed by the time they make contact with the mental health professional.

Concluding Remarks

The disturbed foster or adoptive child has experienced early-on in his life, treatment from caregivers which was abusive, neglectful and/or exploitive. This early exposure to maltreatment shapes this unfortunate child's view of the caregivers and teaches him maladaptive ways of interacting in the family. At the time of placement in the foster or adoptive home, the child is poorly equipped to accept "normal" family life with its insistence on communication, cooperation, agreed-upon rules, solid parent-child boundaries, and intimacy. The child's "black-and-blueprint" of the world cautions him against trust, honesty and love, which is at the core of healthy family life. Many exasperated, somewhat defeated foster and adoptive parents have bemoaned the fact that despite their best efforts the disturbed child refuses to become a functioning member of the family. How can we reach the child who so obstinately resists help? How can we connect with the child who sets us up to reject him? How can we infuse some energy into a child whose earliest months and years of maltreatment have left him lifeless and "old before his time?" We will address these and other questions, as we turn to a discussion of treatment.

"During the first half of this century, clinicians were trained to avoid planning or initiating what was to happen in therapy and to wait for the patient to say or do something...The clinician was expected to sit passively and only interpret or reflect back to a patient what he was saying and doing. He could also offer only one approach no matter how different the kinds of people or problems were that came to him. It was considered 'manipulative' to focus on a problem, set goals, deliberately intervene in a person's life, or examine the results of such therapy."

Jay Haley

4 | The Goals and Objectives of Treatment

T he preceding chapters described foster and adoptive parents who are "up to their necks" with the difficult challenges of raising disturbed children. This chapter will address the goals and objectives of treatment interventions designed to meet those challenges.

Disturbed foster and adoptive children present such a multiplicity of problems that it is mind-boggling to know where to begin an attempt to turn things around in their lives. Chapter 4 will summarize the specific goals and global objectives which give order to an otherwise overwhelming situation. (These are the goals and objectives which underlie the intervention strategies to be discussed in Chapters Five and Six ahead.)

The Goals Behind the Strategies

Simply stated, the four goals of treatment strategies with disturbed foster and adoptive children are:

- Containing the acting-out behavior which undermines the stabililty of placement.
- Increasing the child's verbalization of his underlying mental blueprint of the world, caregivers and himself.
- Fostering the child's ability to negotiate with others for the purpose of meeting his needs.
- Promoting positive encounters which provide an opportunity for increased attachment in the foster or adoptive family.

> *"Acting-out behavior can quickly set up a situation in which the foster or adoptive parents are frightened, enraged, defeated and paralyzed emotionally."*

Containing Acting-Out Behavior

The importance of getting a handle on behavior problems cannot be over-emphasized, as acting-out behavior can quickly set up a situation in which the foster or adoptive parents are frightened, enraged, defeated and paralyzed emotionally. Acting-out behavior is the child's time-worn way of expressing otherwise unresolved and suppressed insecurity, grief and anger towards the world, himself, siblings and caregivers. This behavior distances new caregivers and undermines offers of intimacy, connection and caring. In short order, acting-out behavior sets the stage for negative parental reactions which are hauntingly familiar to the child yet puzzling and upsetting to the foster or adoptive parents. In effect, they become characters in the child's past drama. In the words of Yogi Berra—the baseball legend—"It's like deja vu all over again." The "deja vu" experience traps new parent figures in a reenactment of old relationships. In quick order, the placement is in deep jeopardy, as in the following case:

* * * * *

Bobby, a passive, overly compliant eight-year-old adopted boy, wore an almost constant, blitheful smile on his face. This "game show host" smile masked underlying anxiety following years of maltreatment, rejection and abandonment by his biological mother, grandparents and other relatives. After multiple foster home placements, Bobby was placed in a first-time adoptive home. The unsuspecting adoptive parents thought they could "love Bobby out of his past." However within three weeks of Bobby's placement with them, the adoption, in their own words, was "on the rocks."

In that short span of time, the adoptive parents had been worn out by Bobby's bottomless needs. He shadowed their every move. Too frightened to sleep alone, he crawled in bed with them. Nightly dreams about monsters, killings and being left alone haunted Bobby. During the day he seemed unable to entertain himself and needed constant direction. Bobby was a hodgepodge of worries, fears and dependencies.

The adoptive mother could not even go to the bathroom without Bobby sitting on the other side of the door. If she attempted to leave him to talk to a neighbor across the street, Bobby dogged her every step. His motto seemed to be, "Bobby—don't leave home without me."

In a matter of a few weeks, the adoptive parents felt physically depleted and emotionally drained by Bobby's relentless demands, wearily stating, "We are more like babysitters than parents. We can't leave him alone for a minute or he panics, and later we pay for it. . .it's almost too much to deal with."

*   *   *   *   *

A comedienne once stated quite intuitively, that after becoming a mother she understood why some animals eat their young. Many exasperated foster and adoptive parents reach a similar point of understanding while parenting disturbed children.

In the case of Bobby, containing acting-out behavior was of primary importance in stabilizing his placement and helping him work through his serious emotional problems. His negative past experiences with caregivers had rendered him anxious and insecure in all subsequent relationships. In the adoptive home Bobby clearly expected to be rejected, left behind and abandoned once again. His clinging, overanxious behaviors overwhelmed the adoptive parents, who then came close to rejecting and abandoning him. Subconsciously, Bobby had set up a pattern of interaction which deprived him of what he so badly needed. Without decisive, strategic therapeutic interventions, the placement was almost over before it had a chance.

Increasing Verbalization

A focus solely on containing acting-out behavior without working simultaneously on other goals would result in failure. Volumes have been written cautioning against "symptom substitution," which occurs when we try to merely stamp out "bad behavior" without working on underlying causes. In cases of disturbed foster/adoptive children, the underlying pressures for acting-out are the child's negative view of the world—especially of caregivers—and unresolved issues concerning loss, insecurity, intimacy, rejection, grief and rage.

The second goal of intervention strategies is to encourage and prompt the child to verbalize his underlying perceptions, feelings and views of the world, himself and caregivers. If the child expresses his negative

"Unless the child gains the ability to articulate what he feels, he lives a life of denial, repression, avoidance, and guardedness."

blueprint behaviorally, the placement will continue to be in turmoil, his inner pain will not be alleviated, and he will not learn to open up and express his feelings. Unless the child gains the ability to articulate what he feels, he lives a life of denial, repression, avoidance and guardedness. Pathetically, without an "emotional voice box" the child is kept away from those who—given half a chance—could soothe his pain, reduce his anger and fill his emptiness, as seen in the next case example:

* * * * *

Herbert was a tall, good-looking fourteen-year-old who had lived in relative stability and harmony with his adoptive parents during his ten years in their home. Following a brief period of early clingingness and insecurity, Herbert had ostensibly thrived with his adoptive family. However, after a serious illness which hospitalized the adoptive mother for two weeks, Herbert's behavior sharply deteriorated: he lied, was truant from school and was arrested for drunkenness and fighting with the arresting officer. Herbert refused to visit his mother during her hospitalization and afterwards seemed very cold and uncommunicative.

In taking the history—both distant and more recent—what came to light was the extent of the losses Herbert had experienced as a young child prior to coming to live with his adoptive family. Herbert, though not "unattached," had remained "loss sensitive" over the years. While he had lived in relative family bliss with this solid adoptive family, his fears of loss of the adoptive mother triggered acting-out. In subsequent family sessions, the therapist worked with the family to encourage Herbert to vocalize his worst fears about his adoptive mother. Based upon his distant past, Herbert had expected at some preconscious level that ultimately he would be left by her. His compliant behavior over the years in placement had been an attempt to be so meritorious that no one could reject or leave him. When he was "left" by the adoptive mother during her hosptilization, he was terrified and enraged. Hence, the uncharacteristic acting-out behavior.

Over time Herbert began to express his underlying fears and assumptions about mothers directly to his adoptive mother and father. Once these "unspeakable" emotions and perceptions were uttered out-

loud, the pressure to act-out was alleviated.

* * * * *

This case typifies how vocalization of the feelings, thoughts, perceptions and issues—harbored in the negative mental blueprint—reduces the child's need for "behavioralizing" underlying conflicts, distortions and fears. It bears repeating here that without working simultaneously in our interventions on both the containment of acting-out and the verbalization of the negative mental blueprint, we are primed for failure.

Fostering Negotiation Skills

To function adequately in social encounters, individuals—with their idiosyncratic thoughts, perceptions, feelings, needs, ambitions and goals—rely heavily on their ability to negotiate with others. Rarely do human beings share identical desires and motivations, and yet they find themselves required to interact, live, grow, work and love together. People must negotiate with each other to function well interpersonally.

The disturbed foster or adoptive child typically has poor negotiation skills or abhors negotiation altogether. Having been raised in a maltreating environment, his needs, perceptions, thoughts and feelings were misunderstood, disregarded, ridiculed or otherwise punished. The dysfunctional family setting in which he was reared early-on convinced him that his needs and ambitions were unimportant or undesirable. Over time, this young child developed solitary ways of meeting his needs. Gradually he adapted to the unfeeling, insensitive, unreliable and unresponsive caregiving in his abusive, neglectful or exploitive home. In short, he took care of himself as best he could. While serving a purpose in his family of origin, later in the foster or adoptive home, "survival behaviors" were unneeded and harmful, as seen in the following case:

* * * * *

Franklin, a frail five-year-old Caucasian boy, was adopted after three prior foster home placements. Superficially compliant, Franklin was a passive, peaceable but quietly vengeful boy with many secret ways of meeting his needs. A quick inspection of Franklin's history revealed exposure to frightening episodes of child abuse and domestic violence. Franklin had been, for example, kidnapped by his cocaine-addicted biological father during an incident of domestic violence. He had witnessed his father pummel his mother unconscious on several occasions; he observed his father put a gun to her head twice; and on one occasion he witnessed his drug-crazed father break down the front door to the house to get at his hysterical, cowering wife.

In the midst of all this, Franklin had learned to survive by taking a "low profile." But he had not been totally spared his father's mercurial violence. As a crying infant, Franklin had been thrown against the wall twice by his father, once sustaining a skull fracture. A fairly active and feisty toddler, he had been cuffed and back-handed, according to the mother. Ultimately Franklin learned to avoid his father and to "read" his moods. Since speaking up, fighting back or complaining was so dangerous, he learned to keep silent. Franklin never expressed discontent, desire or difference of opinion around his father. Instead he learned "maladaptive" ways of coping with harsh reality. That is, his needs went underground but did not disappear altogether. So too, were his anger and frustration submerged.

Franklin brought his expectations about caregivers, especially male caregivers, into each new foster or adoptive home. Along with this "negative mental blueprint," Franklin brought his characteristic, "maladaptive" patterns of behavior, his sneaky, underground ways of satisfying his needs. Nowhere in his past had he learned to deal directly with caregivers about the meeting of his needs, nor had he learned to work out differences of opinion. He operated on the assumption that he would have to meet his wants and desires by himself. In adoptive care Franklin was a highly skilled thief and an accomplished liar. The stealing stemmed from his belief that he must take what he needed, that it would not be supplied by parent figures. The lying was based upon his perception that caregivers would be harsh in their punishments if he spoke his true thoughts and feelings.

The adoptive family stated that they wished that Franklin would trust them and would confront, assert or express himself and his wishes. They added that their biological son, age four, was already masterful in his ability to identify, express and fight for what he wanted. Clearly, to reach Franklin the adoptive parents would have to elicit and contain his negative behavior, to increase his verbalizing and to teach him that needs could be met through relationships (through negotiation).

* * * * *

It is commonly assumed that healthy relationships are based on "give and take" ("I give and you take, then, you give and I take.") However, to the disturbed child, relationships mean either giving up or taking all you can get. Thus, the questions arise: How can we convince these youngsters to enter into a true give-and-take relationship? How can we show that we understand their unique thoughts, needs, ambitions and goals? How can we convince them that we want to help them to meet their needs, even when they are not identical to our own? How can we persuade them to bargain, negotiate, compromise and debate with us?

"To the disturbed child, relationships mean either giving up or taking all you can get."

Promoting Positive Encounters

The fourth goal of treatment of the disturbed child is promoting positive encounters with him. These are the encounters which the formerly maltreated foster or adoptive child has experienced too sparsely or irregularly in his earlier years. Positive encounters include holding, hugging, comforting, nurturing, feeding, protecting, communicating, laughing together, listening to, stimulating and disciplining—all when the child needs them. These are activities which serve to engage the child in mutually fulfilling encounters, and ultimately lead the child to feeling wanted, safe and confident. We want the child to start believing that parent figures are responsive, available and able to meet his needs. Positive encounters—in adoption—permit the caregivers to "claim" the child in a forceful, loving way. In both foster and adoptive work, positive encounters provide the child with a sense of importance and belongingness. Overall such encounters propel the child toward intimacy, trusting emotional connections and a secure affectional bond or attachment to the foster or adoptive parents.

"Positive encounters provide the child with a sense of importance and belongingness."

Unfortunately, positive encounters are absent for the child when caregivers neglect, abuse or exploit him. They are also absent when the disturbed child clings to his maladaptive behavior, to his negative blueprint; that is, when he rejects the outstretched hand or "bites that hand" as it attempts to feed him physically and emotionally. His negative view of the world and his maladaptive patterns of interacting conspire against positive encounters in the foster and adoptive home, as seen in the following illustration:

* * * * *

Bert, age 12, was a "whirling dervish" in his adoptive home. This agitated and agitating boy had "two personalities" according to the parents: one was engaging, delightful, loving and witty; the other, hostile, critical, explosive and moody. The adoptive parents reported that Bert would take one step forward, then two steps back. Just when they thought they were getting somewhere with him—feeling good for a few days or a week—Bert would undermine progress and "pull the rug out from under them." At those times his negative behavior would escalate, and he became loud, bossy, explosive and increasingly hyperactive. The willy-nilly pattern of short-lived gains followed by inevitable backsliding exasperated and discouraged the adoptive parents. They seemed further exhausted by Bert's hyperactive behavior, which existed during good times and bad.

* * * * *

There are a myriad of ways in which disturbed children thwart positive encounters. Some are conscious and deliberate, others are unconscious and unplanned. In the case of Bert, they were a little of each. Bert's early history of multiple caregivers, abject neglect and unfortunate series of failed foster home placements left him mistrustful and phobic of the intimacy of family life. His negative expectations about love relationships were confirmed by each successive loss or failure. In time Bert actively precipitated the rejection he perceived as inevitable. His active role in the ruination of his later placements gave him a curious and perverse sense of control in his life and undoubtedly relieved his mounting anxieties over the impending losses he awaited in each foster family. Essentially, he played a game of "let me reject you first." Instead of "waiting for the other shoe to drop," Bert grabbed the shoe figuratively and threw it out the window.

In this case, as in many foster/adoptive placements, Bert had more than psychological problems to contend with. What became evident to his psychologist was that Bert's agitation, anxieties, hyperactivity and explosiveness had a partly physiological cause. A visit to a psychiatrist revealed that Bert suffered from attention deficit hyperactivity disorder—a condition marked by concentration problems, impulsivity and hyperactivity. Once treated with medication, Bert's behavior problems were lessened measurably, giving some immediate relief to his exhausted adoptive parents. Medical management along with more proactive attempts on the part of the adoptive parents to engage Bert positively resulted in a dramatic increase in the stability of the placement.

(We have found that increasing numbers of foster and adoptive children exhibit medical/psychiatric problems which compound or underlie their emotional/behavioral/interpersonal difficulties. With the avalanche of "drug babies" and the ever-increasing numbers of children with "fetal alcohol syndrome," there will be more foster/adoptive children with neurological and neurochemical problems. In many of these cases, medical/psychiatric management can be a helpful adjunct to interventions.)

Some Further Objectives

Beyond the four specific goals of treatment, there are general objectives which guide the development and implementation of our interventions with disturbed foster and adoptive children. They are:

- Taking a proactive rather than reactive approach to the special problems of the disturbed child.
- Injecting levity, spontanaeity and creativity into parenting.
- Intervening in a "team" fashion.
- Focusing on the family as the primary agent of change.

Proactive Parenting

In short order, many foster and adoptive families find themselves "on the ropes" after placement of a disturbed child. Some of these children are simply too much for the typical family to handle. In an all-too-familiar scenario, the child plays the tune and the family dances. Frequently, the parents find themselves stuck in a "reactionary" mode with the child. They often tell us, "This child must lie awake all night dreaming up ways to spoil this placement...to drive us away." In actuality, the child's misbehavior comes naturally, without nighttime premeditation. Ironically, it is the parents who lie awake all night. Proactive parenting permits the parents to get a step ahead of the child and to anticipate problems before they overwhelm the placement.

The family must reframe and re-think their help to the child, to stand back from the constant "brush fires" to find the source of the blaze. With specific goals in mind, they must make an effort to push, coerce, surprise and keep the child from "playing the same old tune."

The Place of Levity, Spontanaeity and Creativity

In response to seemingly never-ending problems, family distress and struggles over control, what little enjoyment is available in parenting the disturbed child fritters away. The seriousness of parenting these children leaves the family bogged down in emotional quick-sand with no help in sight. Moreover many of the interventions used with disturbed children have the net effect of stealing the most important "tool" that parents have with these children—namely, themselves. For example, some behavioral approaches relegate parents to the colorless role of "accountant," rotely recording data while the child takes on the role of "psychic attorney," exploiting loopholes in the system.

Oftentimes levity, spontanaeity and creativity can "save the day" in work with disturbed children. And, we must not forget the power of novelty in working with children who have mastered the "same-old-same-old" existence of expected negative interactions. An example of the unexpected approach is found in the story about a police officer who came upon a man attempting suicide by jumping off a bridge. The officer, surprising himself and the man, instantly drew his revolver and shouted, "Stop, or I'll shoot!" Stunned, the man raised his arms above his head and backed away from the edge. Similarly humor and spontanaeity give us the "ammo" to force the child to consider something other than "emotional suicide." Truly, for many disturbed children human relationships are a life-or-death struggle; they do not know how to laugh, to be joyful and to enjoy others' company. Further, they are figuratively perched on the bridge, bent on self-destruction. In such cases, levity and spontanaeity can surprise the child and cause him to back away from the "edge."

The Team Approach

There is often an unnecessary, irrelevant and counterproductive boundary between therapist, caseworkers and the family. Many traditional interventions focus in one of two directions: one, individual psychotherapy of the child with token consultation to the parents; and two, family therapy that has a "submerged" goal of smoking out problems in the parents or in their marriage. In the former case, the oft-times well-intended therapist unwittingly undermines the placement through efforts at forming an exclusive "special relationship" with the child. Involvement with the parents is reduced to informing them about the highlights of therapeutic progress. In the latter case (in family therapy), treatment is directed away from the problem child and onto the parents (foster/adoptive) as the core of the problem. With disturbed children such approaches are myopic and amount to a "prescription for failure." We have often heard, much to our chagrin, that psychotherapy was successful right up to the time that the placement failed—a failure in fact which is laid on the already hunched shoulders of the beleaguered parents.

Overanalyzing of the parents and solo treatment of the child are hazardous in the special situation of disturbed foster and adoptive children. Faced with the task of parenting and treating the formerly maltreated child, it is critical that all forces come together. The inherent differences and distrust that often underlie the relationships between and among the family, agencies and professionals must be put aside.

We have found that a therapeutic team comprised of mental health professional, family, caseworker and school personnel—all striving with unified goals—has great synergistic power.[2] That is, their helping impact is greater than the sum of individual parts. In a collaborative approach, they are less apt to be "split" apart from each other by the child's attempts to ally with some and to reject others. The acknowledgement and support of members of the team can inflate deflated parents, offer support and advice, and, in a sense, innoculate them against "imported pathology."

The Family As Primary Agent of Change

There is not a school teacher, nor a therapist, nor a friendly neighbor, nor any other well-intended individual that can make the difference in the disturbed child's life the way his family can. (In many instances this is the foster and adoptive family. However, sometimes this may also involve the biological family, in situations where they are still an active part of the child's life.) While many individuals can have a positive place in the child's world, the changes each can make are at times secondary. It is the moment-by-moment, interaction-by-interaction, day-to-day struggles that primarily lead to the building of bonds, the mitigation of past injuries and abuses and the re-socialization of the child. Given the importance of the family—foster or adoptive—it is mandatory that they be supported, nurtured, respected and recognized for their primary role in treatment of the child.

Concluding Remarks

This chapter reviewed the major goals and objectives behind treatment of the disturbed child. These goals and objectives are the foundation upon which helpful interventions can be constructed. Many disturbed foster and adoptive children often fail to respond to conventional interventions. In fact, some traditional approaches may interfere inadvertently with the stability of foster and adoptive placements. Treatment failures occur most often if the foster and adoptive parents are excluded from the "treatment team." In our view, foster and adoptive parents are the key members of the treatment team and must be integrally involved in the design and implementaton of treatment strategies.

Having discussed the maltreated child, his negative impact on the foster and adoptive family and the goals and objectives of treatment, we move to a detailed presentation of unconventional strategies.

5 Unconventional Strategies for Containing Acting-Out and Increasing Verbalization

T he first group of strategies—eleven in number—which will be described and explained in this chapter, address the first two goals of treatment: containing acting-out behavior and increasing verbalization.

Overview of Strategies

Table 5.1 lists eleven strategies which focus upon either containing acting-out behavior or increasing verbalization as a primary goal.

Table 5.1 Unconventional Strategies

1. The "Unending Pizza" Strategy.
2. Creating A Catastrophy.
3. Infantalizing.
4. The "Steal Thyself Blind" Strategy.
5. The "Not Now I Have A Headache" Strategy.
6. A "Dose of Reality" Strategy.
7. The "Sargeant Carter Approach."
8. The "Mayor Arne Nilsen Rule."
9. The "Perseverating Penance" Strategy.
10. The "Line in the Sand" Approach.
11. "Feelings 101".

In this chapter each strategy will be presented with the following format: (a) a brief description of the subject or problem area; (b) the major goal(s) addressed by the strategy; (c) an explanation of the strategy through case discussion; (d) remarks about the case and the intervention; and (e) a question and answer section.

NOTE: We feel obliged to point out that by enumeration of these various strategies, we do not endorse a "cookbook" approach to handling disturbed children. Nor do we mean to imply that intervention with seriously disturbed children only entails the application of certain clever techniques. Instead, we hope that the following strategies will provide examples of how we conceptualize and systematically address serious, "stickey wicket" quandries which appear in foster and adoptive placements. Additionally, the description of these strategies will hopefully provide a framework for designing future interventions which are appropriate, yet creative and proactive for other children in other families. Development of any serious treatment strategies is best done in the context of the "treatment team;" unconventional strategies should be fitting to the child's age—chronological and psychological—and should be sensitive to his present needs, history, experience of trauma and his rights as a young human being. It should go without saying that the strategies should never be used vindictively or with cruel intent. Lastly, the strategies should be developed and employed to comply with relevant state laws and regulations regarding children.

1 The "Unending Pizza" Strategy

Subject:

• Children with eating disorders

Major Goals:

• Containing acting-out behaviors
• Fostering negotiation skills

One way that children reflect their emotional disturbance is through disorders in patterns of eating. Some gorge, purge, refuse to eat and grapple in endless, self-destructive power struggles over sustenance. Others steal and hide food, play with their food for hours, or engage in such bizarre behaviors as eating out of the dog's dish. Such eating problems often relate to past family experiences and are later used for "hidden purposes" within current relationships.

For the disturbed child, eating provides an arena for playing out old power struggles and re-living past pathological caretaking. Eating disorders demonstrate the child's lack of awareness of needs and historic discomfort at mealtime—due to negative past experiences around the table. As mealtimes can imply intimacy, some children do what they can to be removed from the unspoken demand for closeness. Children who have not had basic sustenance needs provided for distrust that they will be given what they need and perceive that they must go "underground" to meet their own needs. For some children eating provides the only satisfying way to meet twisted emotional needs. While some youngsters refuse to eat, others exert unbending control over what they will eat, when they will eat and with whom.

Parents and other caregivers attempt to handle eating problems through a variety of interventions—mostly behavioral programs that reinforce or punish. Unfortunately, behavioristic attempts are often ineffective because of deeper issues concealed by the eating disturbance. For instance, eating "misbehavior" may be a way in which the child exerts control over self as well as control over caregiving and nurturing relationships.

In cases that fail to respond to traditional interventions due to this rigid control and a struggle for power by the child, the "Unending Pizza Strategy" offers some "food for thought." Consider the following:

* * * * *

Sally was driving her foster parents crazy with her nightly battles at the dinner table. This child, a formerly abused and neglected eight-year-old, would sit for hours staring at her dinner plate. The doctor's office expressed concern about her poor eating habits and nutrition, though her weight and height were average. It turned out that Sally had discovered a secret cache of food—

"He asked them to side-step suppertime struggles."

namely, pizza kept in the freezer in the garage. She had covertly gnawed through three large pepperoni pizzas. Her physician humorously diagnosed this as a rare case of "Rodentia Italiana," that is to say, "Italian Rodent Syndrome." In truth, Sally had serious emotional/ behavioral problems related to her unyielding power struggles at the table. Nothing the foster parents tried helped. They coaxed, pleaded, and threatened—all to no avail. Sally continued to hunch over her plate for hours, refusing to eat regular meals. Of course she had been eating the pizza on the sly.

The psychologist encouraged the family to side-step suppertime struggles, as it was determined that the more strongly they attempted to intervene or coerce the child, the more vigorously she resisted. The "Unending Pizza Strategy" was employed at this point. Sally had her dream come true. She was given pizza for breakfast, lunch and dinner—presented with kindness and a smile. If she wanted it cold, she got it cold. If she wanted it warmed, she got it warmed. Sally was, in effect, given exactly what she wanted—total control over her diet. The family continued to eat their regular meals, along side of the "Rodentia Italiana." Within six weeks Sally was asking for what they were eating.

* * * * *

Why did this strategy work with Sally? Because it gave her total control, side-stepped her historic use of food as a battleground and allowed her—on her own terms and without a power struggle—to discover what her body needed and what she truly wanted—a variety of nutritious, good-tasting food. A significant side-effect of the "Unending Pizza Strategy" was that Sally participated in the family meal for the very first time.

We might add here that a family's handling of this type of situation takes a certain amount of willingness to be creative and unusual (to let go of the "time-tested" ways of solving problems) and a belief in allowing children to assert their needs, even in bizarre ways—at least temporarily. Note here that in order to heighten the impact of this strategy and to allow Sally a feeling of control, the family needs to "reluctantly" allow the child to participate in regular meals. For example, when Sally, after six weeks of pizza tentatively asked for a piece of pie for dessert, the foster mother did not gush with excitement, at least on the outside; instead, she suggested that perhaps Sally had not had enough pizza, cutting her another slice. Ironically, this forced Sally to request—to demand actually—what she wanted. Speaking with a tone of obstinance, Sally remarked, "No, I think I'll have some of that pie tonight. I'm sick of pizza!"

* * * * *

Remarks

Sally, clearly a "mixed type" of maltreated child, certainly presented more behavior problems than her obvious eating disorder. Her early history revealed exposure to rigid, abusive, totalitarian parenting. For instance, Sally had been forced to sit for hours at a time until she finished every morsel on her plate. In the face of tyrannical parenting approaches, Sally could not voice her wants, her frustration and her will. Her battles with her earliest caregivers then became covert. And eating was not the only vehicle of conflict. Sally also was engaged in a covert war over toileting and personal hygiene—other issues surrounding the control of her body.

Once placed in foster care with a relatively permissive, democratic family, Sally might have been expected to drop old behavior problems and attitudes. However, the "black-and-blueprint" closed her eyes to the new view of life presented in this home. In fact, Sally clung staunchly to her old, negative view of caregivers and behaved accordingly.

The goals of the "Unending Pizza Strategy" were to free Sally from her historical battles which were now maladaptive in the new home (containing acting-out behavior). It strove to illustrate and prove to her that there is "give-and-take" in a parent-child relationship; that the child can state needs and preferences to the parent with the expectation that the caregiver will listen and respond (increasing verbalizations); that Sally could relinquish the stubborn tendency to control and permit a benevolent parent figure to be in charge; and ultimately, that she could allow herself to be parented.[3]

Questions and Answers

1. Some foster and adoptive parents ask, "Do we have to run a short-order cafe for our kids? Wouldn't the other kids want pizza, too?"

Our experience has shown that the "contagion effect" is very short-lived. Children without the recalcitrant power struggles over food quickly drop their obsession when allowed a few pizza meals in a row.

2. How can simply getting a child to change an eating habit have much of an effect on her deeper emotional problems?

By getting her "unstuck," we have an opportunity to connect with her and to reduce her conflicts around the dinner table, which we can extend to other areas of her life. We need to understand her "negative mental blueprint" and must contain such destructive acting-out if we are to help her change.

3. What happens if Sally continues to want to eat that one thing? Aren't we taking a chance on her health? Why continue if that's possible?

If it doesn't work, don't use it. The child's doctor of course can monitor health concerns. If the situation is intractable despite the use of this strategy, there are other approaches to reducing the acting-out and to encouraging verbalization of the underlying "mental blueprint," discussed in other sections of this book.

4. What other eating problems might respond to novel strategies?

Two other problems come to mind: one, the younger child (preschooler) who refuses to eat much of anything and who shows no clear preference for one special food; and two, the preschool or school-aged child who gorges food, eating anything and everything.

Briefly, with the first case the foster or adoptive parents might try sitting the child on their lap and spoon or bottle feeding the child, as if he were an infant. This might circumvent negative-attention-seeking while soldering the connection between eating and loving, nurturant caregiving.

In the second case (the "gorger"), wherein the child steals food in order to eat wolfishly in private, again the use of close parent contact is crucial. In this instance the parent might sit the younger child on her lap and feed him with baby utensils, insisting on eye contact between each bite. The tiny utensils slow the pace of "wolfing" food, while lengthening the amount of lap time the parent has with the child.

* * * * *

2 Creating A Catastrophy

Subject:

• Children who overdramatize their problems

Major Goal:

• Containing acting-out

Many foster and adoptive parents find that their child occasionally becomes overdramatic, hysterical and makes catastrophies out of small problems and frustrations to get attention or to manipulate. Some of these children learn early-on to throw horrendous temper tantrums or to "turn on the tears" as a way of getting what they want at the moment. As these children grow older, their manipulation through theatrics may become more sophisticated. In our attempts to help and remove pain, we often rush in, deceived by their award-winning performance, inadvertantly reinforcing the behavior, as in the following case:

* * * * *

Brandon, a clever thirteen-year-old adopted boy, ran down the hall and slammed the door to his room so hard that the windows shook.

"Nobody loves me! You all hate me. I might as well kill myself!" he screamed at the top of his lungs. The adoptive mother, Mrs. T., was hooked. Hurrying down to the room, quite alarmed, she tried to open the door, but Brandon had barracaded himself in his room. "I hate you all! I hate myself! I don't want to live anymore!" He raged on. Mrs. T. pleaded with Brandon to open the door, to no avail. Then she attempted in her most soothing voice to calm and reassure him, "We do too love you, Brandon. You mean a lot to us. You are our son." "No I'm not...I'm adopted and you know it!" was his retort. Mrs. T. felt compelled to dissuade Brandon of this feeling; her efforts went on for a solid hour through the door.

*   *   *   *   *

Children like Brandon play on our natural sympathies for foster and adoptive children who have had such horrendous backgrounds. They play on our insecurities and guilt as well: "Are we doing enough? Are we loving enough? Maybe we truly don't feel like Brandon is ours." The theatrics serve a purpose: to keep us working hard and to keep us on a negative attention pathway with the child. All the while that we are responding to these shinanigans, we are left with less opportunity to connect in healthy ways with the child. We are marching to the beat of his drum. To counter this, the strategy of "Creating A Catastrophy" seems to work well, as seen below:

*   *   *   *   *

Mrs. T., having conferred with the psychologist, was prepared for the next explosive episode; it wasn't a long wait. Brandon made a big scene on his birthday, though he was given more presents than he had ever received in his life. "Bobby (his brother) will get more presents on his birthday than I got!" Brandon began to escalate, becoming more irrational, as usual. Instead of attempting to calm him down (which would only serve to pour gasoline on the fire), Mrs. T. marched off to the kitchen. In a few minutes she started talking to herself in a louder and louder voice, "Nobody appreciates what I do around here! I try to buy presents

"Why doesn't someone appreciate me as a mother?"

and nobody likes them! Why even buy anything? Why doesn't someone appreciate me as a mother?" Just for effect, she rattled pots and pans together and closed the cabinet doors with a force. After about five minutes, she noticed that Brandon had stopped yelling. In another minute, he was peering tentatively around the corner of the kitchen, "What's the matter, Mom?" he asked.

* * * * *

We might just as easily name this approach the "Snuffing Out Oil Fires" strategy. As you may know, oil well fire-fighters put out raging infernos with an explosion of their own. The detonation near the burning oil well smothers the fire by robbing it of available oxygen. Certainly, at times our best efforts at putting out explosive situations via understanding, soothing, comforting and so on actually make things worse. Indeed, Bobby found soothing words more irritating and provoking than comforting. When others attempted to lend him their support, he went ballistic. Perhaps he had learned that his "temper tantrums" would alarm others and extort from them what he wanted. Or maybe he simply had never learned to take charge of his temper, putting the responsibility on others to curb his volatility. Whatever the cause, the effect of his anger was to distance and control others.

The unexpected, uncharacteristic response by the adoptive mother, put Brandon off his stride. It had the effect of jarring him out of his usual spiraling out of control. Mrs. T.'s "outburst" had a way of upstaging her manipulative son.

Remarks

Brandon was a boy with "mixed type" symptoms: he was at times antisocial in his manipulation and explosive temper; at other times he appeared overanxious/insecure and prone to hysteria.

In his family of origin, Brandon's combination of symptoms had apparently functioned to keep him in the limelight; it also served to get him his way, as his inadequate mother responded to guilt-inducing, panic-peddling sound and fury.

Generally in foster and adoptive care, new parent figures attempt to persuade the child that he/she can receive love, affection and attention by normal means; that he does not have to go through wacky gyrations to secure some modicum of human approbation. However, some children are so disturbed and have learned only convoluted ways of extorting attention from adults. Though these old ways are maladaptive and unnecessary, these youngsters compulsively repeat them in the foster or adoptive home.

Questions and Answers

1. Is an approach like this do-able with younger children?

Yes. Irritating as tantrums may be, we have known foster families who do not easily knuckle under when their younger-aged foster children "pitch a conniption fit." One such family would gather around the child and watch rather than ignore the fit. The angry foster child quickly discovered that his temper tantrum was to no avail. In one adoptive home the father would lie down on the floor next to the child and yell and scream along with him. Again, the child seemed to lose interest in this negative approach to getting his way.

2. Aren't we setting a bad example for the child by becoming hysterical ourselves?

If we were to pitch fits about our own issues on a regular basis, this would indeed model immature, maladaptive behavior. However, the objective of this strategy is to disrupt the child's outburst by our outlandish, ludicrous, up-staging behavior.

3. What about alternatives to this approach?

Yes. Instead of creating a catastrophe the foster or adoptive parent may allow the child to "have his catastrophe" his own way. One family found their eleven-year-old adoptive son frequently packing his bags whenever he grew frustated in the placement. "Nobody cares about me, anyway," he would complain. "I might as well move out." In place of creating a catastrophe, the adoptive mother would quietly bring out the suitcase and lay it on the child's bed. "We sure will miss you, if you go," she lamented. This approach effectively neutralized the boy's histrionic ploy. His expectation was that someone would attempt to dissuade him from going. Instead, he was faced with making his own decision about whether he should remain in his adoptive family.[4]

* * * * *

3 Infantalizing

Subject:

- Regressed, helpless, whiney, negative-attention-seeking children who refuse to grow up

Major Goal:

- Containing acting-out

Infantalizing (babying or allowing the child to regress) can be a helpful adjunct to work with seriously disturbed foster and adoptive children. Ironically, treating the child as if he were younger can propel him to act older, as seen in the next case illustration:

* * * * *

"Why don't you act your age?"

Tabatha was a resistant, oppositional ten-year-old adopted girl with a sad history of multiple losses, abandonment, neglect and "foster care drift." In this her second adoptive attempt, Tabatha was doing poorly according to the discouraged parents. After twelve months in the adoptive home, finalization had not occured since the adoptive parents were finding Tabatha oftentimes too unpleasant, distant and passive-resistant. Though they could not pinpoint any single remarkable problem, Tabatha was experienced as totally unrewarding, emotionally draining and immature. In a moment of frustration, the adoptive mother stated, "She is driving us crazy with her stubbornness and her refusal to grow up...she will not pick up after herself, she still battles us over what she will wear, and she acts as if she can't do anything for herself...She is draining us dry...you just want to ask her, 'Why don't you act your age?'"

The psychologist found that the adoptive parents had (initially in the placement) attempted to push Tabatha towards maturity too quickly. Immediately upon placement they identified her as lagging behind emotionally, socially and intellectually. In their urge to help Tabatha, they instituted structured homework time, insisted that she dress herself appropriately, and directed her to do chores like their younger birth children were doing already. Tabatha balked, resisted and rebelled—silently—in the face of this "programmed maturation" approach. Much of her passive-resistance was in response to perceived coercion by the

78

adoptive parents. Given Tabatha's mental image of parents as neglectful of her needs, she felt that the adoptive parents were insensitive to what she was ready for and what she needed. Her characteristic response had been to foot-drag, undermine and resist in the face of such perceived insensitivity by caregivers. Not surprisingly, she responded to the adoptive parents in a similar fashion.

The psychological strategy in this case was to infantalize Tabatha and to meet her at a much younger emotional level. The adoptive parents devised some approaches that they could feel at least relatively comfortable in using with Tabatha. For example, they agreed to rock her daily in their arms—despite her fairly large size for a ten-year-old. They also bottle-fed her, using juices or chocolate milk (Tabatha's favorite beverages). The most difficult strategy for the adoptive parents involved dropping chores, room clean-up, and the insistence upon Tabatha picking out her own clothes and dressing herself.

* * * * *

In the case of Tabatha, as with many children who act rebelliously in response to the demands of maturity, the infantalizing approach can reduce power struggles over growth and maturation. It also can relieve the adoptive or foster parent of the sense of urgency to assist the child in moving upwards along the developmental growth curve. This approach is ideal for children who "dig in their heels" over issues regarding maturation. Their general immaturity, emotional neediness and unmet dependency needs prevent them from developing like more normal children. Instead of insisting on their "right" to grow up, these children expend a great deal of energy "staying small."

Along with the "stay small" mentality of some seriously disturbed foster and adoptive children, there is a corresponding tendency on the part of good adoptive and foster parents to want to correct this problem expeditously. Sensing the child's immaturity, adoptive (or foster) parents set about the task of moving the child forward. Unfortunately the passive-resistant, emotionally-needy child often views attempts to help him grow up as hasty, threatening, callous to his needs and evidence of adult insensitivity. His response is to move in the opposite direction of parental force; that is, he regresses, becomes more immature, helpless and inadequate.

Stepping back for a moment, let us examine what we are trying to accomplish. With the infantalizing strategy we attempt to move paradoxically in the direction of the child's inner need to "stay small." For example, with Tabatha we rock and bottle-feed her—not to humiliate or denigrate her in any way and certainly not to punish her. In addition, we might help her with the clothes selection, help her button her shirt, zip her zippers and tie her shoes. These all are infantalizing strategies which go beyond what Tabatha has ever asked for (or perhaps beyond what she has even dreamed). With this approach we make it possible for Tabatha to eventually "demand" to grow up. After receiving from the adoptive parents a liberal amount of coddling, protection and babying, Tabatha eventually comes to the point of saying, "me do it"—words spoken by toddlers who are well cared for, fawned over and loved. These normal tots, pressed from within by the natural yearning to mature, insist that their parents give them some room to grow up. "Me do it" is what we are looking for Tabatha to say when we stop saying to her—with our behavior and words—"**you** do it."

Remarks

From the case above, one can see that Tabatha was an inadequate/dependent child with a passive-resistant streak—a youngster who had been sorely neglected in her earliest years. She was a child whose apathetic biological mother had not wanted her to remain a baby for long, as that would have put an additional burden on her. Over the months and years in the care of this "nominal" parent figure, Tabatha found no reward in the process of maturing. She learned quickly that the faster she grew up, the less she received from her emotionally impoverished mother.

It is important in our work with disturbed foster and adoptive children to assess their developmental ages: physical, cognitive, social and emotional. Those developmental lags which we identify must be addressed in ways that maximize growth and eliminate deficits. Specifically, emotional and social problems arising out of chronic maltreatment are of extreme importance to our therapeutic interventions. It must be remembered—in our urgency to eliminate deficits and maximize growth—that we do not invite staunch resistance. It is crucial with many disturbed children that we meet them "where they are at" developmentally and coax, rather than force, them ahead. With regressed children like Tabatha, we may have more success in holding her back until she insists on moving forward. Often placing the regressed child in the position of insisting on maturation is more productive than pressing her forward against her wishes.

Questions and Answers

1. What if the regressed child merely continues to regress further with this strategy? How long should the strategy be tried before giving up on it?

Further regression may indicate that we have not yet gone far enough back with the child developmentally to connect with him. We may need to actually "overdo it" to a point, so that the child is infantalized past the level that he/she even desires. This may release the child from the power struggle with the adult world.

At times the regression allowed should be circumscribed and limited to situations where the caregivers can truly indulge and infantalize the child. At other moments, the child should be held more closely to age-appropriate behavior.

As for length of trial, this should be determined by the treatment team.

2. Isn't this approach just an example of "reverse psychology" in which we trick the child into doing the opposite of what we say?

Not at all. Reverse psychology implies a clever manipulation of the child, whereas this strategy addresses a deep, oft-times unrecognized developmental arrest of the child. That is, we are meeting needs of the child which—remaining unmet—have checked his progress.

3. What about the child who resists infantalization, though he needs it?

Many children initially react to infantalization with embarrassment, discomfort and resistance. Similarly, the foster or adoptive parents find this strategy to be immediately awkward and unsettling. "This child just needs to grow up!" is the frequently heard reaction of the caregiver. However, once past the initial discomfort, both child and parent may find some inherent rewards in this approach. Children who have never been allowed much "lap time" may revel in the security and warmth of surrendering to positive parental attention.

* * * * *

4 The "Steal Thyself Blind" Strategy

> ### Subject:
> * Children who constantly steal, hoard, and pilfer
>
> ### Major Goals:
> * Containing acting-out behavior
> * Promoting positive encounters

Foster and adoptive parents frequently complain that their child steals.

In the disturbed child, chronic stealing finds its roots in a deep sense of being neglected and feeling forced to take care of himself. An inner void and pessimistic expectation of parent figures drive children to fill the hollowness themselves. Even in foster and adoptive families that offer them "everything," these children will not accept what is offered. Take for example the child who refuses seconds at the dinner table but sneaks a "midnight snack." The compulsion to steal is deeply entrenched and highly resistant to change, as seen in the case below:

* * * * *

Robert, an eight-year-old adopted child from Central America, was an accomplished thief. A timid, withdrawn and non-assertive boy around adult caregivers, he was—in his adoptive mother's words—"a compulsive packrat." Robert could not resist taking any object, small or large. Under Robert's bed the adopted father discovered a large cache of "baubles, bangles and beads"—worthless junk that he had taken from his parents' bedroom, from the other children in the home and from school. The parents were alarmed by the intractable problem of stealing and expected the worst. Specifically, they fretted about Robert ultimately winding up in jail or prison.

Previous efforts to curb the stealing consisted of lectures from the parents, a trip to the minister's office, and lavishing praise for the slightest attempts at honesty. While various interventions fleetingly "helped," stealing inevitably returned. Each apparent gain was cancelled out by the child's return to stealing, leaving the parents feeling angry and dejected: "Why should we try to help him with this problem? Every time he promises to stop, he steals again. . .Just when we seem to be getting somewhere, we find that he has taken something. . .It ruins our trust in him and makes us feel used and 'taken.'"

The psychologist and adoptive parents devised a strategy for addressing the stealing problem in a very different way. With this new plan the adoptive parents took Robert shopping at a discount store for "trinkets," such as miniature cars, model soldiers, plastic molded creatures and erasers—the very things that he loved to steal—matching Robert dollar-for-dollar on his purchase. Next, the parents hid several tantalizing items around the house each day, while Robert was away at school. When Robert returned home, he was challenged to find the hidden items without being caught in the act of "stealing." According to the rules, if he were caught, the items were returned to the parents. Importantly, the parents were then to make a great, humorous fanfare over their success in catching the boy "in the act," and were to chase Robert through the house, yelling "stop thief!" When Robert was seen stealing, the mother or father would chase Robert until they finally cornered him, pinned him down and roughhoused with him, all under the guise of "arresting him." On the other hand, when Robert successfully stole a trinket, he simply kept it. No congratulations were in order and no special attention given. Robert's "petty" thievery gradually diminished.

* * * * *

The "Steal Thyself Blind" strategy was not intended to address stealing directly, but rather to redefine and to take the negativity out of it. Robert was allowed to steal as much as he wanted but only under the terms of the "game" and only from himself. The negativity was neutralized by the parental

"Promoting healthy stealthiness."

permission to "steal." That is, they were promoting healthy stealthiness. This also permitted the adoptive parents to provide more precisely what Robert truly needed—love and affection, physical roughhousing, animated positive interactions and an upbeat, playful family atmosphere.

Before the strategy was employed, the adoptive parents had feared that Robert via his compulsion to steal was a "budding sociopath," destined for a life of crime and punishment. Every missing object was viewed as one more shred of evidence that their worst fears were true. These fears in effect kept them distant and morbidly preoccupied with this child. Indeed, how could the adoptive parents—always vigilant against the "thief"—relax enough to be close and trusting? Perpetually on-guard, they soon neglected the positive aspects to parenting, which in turn only served to confirm Robert's view of parents as stingy with affection.

By devising this new "game," Robert's need for control was respected but was structured in a more prosocial and playful direction. Prior to setting up the "game," spontanaeity, playfulness and intimacy had fallen victim to a deadly parent-child struggle. Redefining the game allowed parents to regain some of the playful, nurturing interactions they had lost soon after placement.

As with many of the unconventional strategies, it is important that the child be placed "off balance," that he not be allowed to play out his sabotaging, destructive patterns—which interfere with closeness, intimacy, and continuity of placement.

Remarks

Robert was an inadequate/dependent adoptive boy whose needs had been chronically neglected early in his life. To Robert the stealing which was so upsetting to the adoptive parents was merely a "replacement" for what he had missed—emotional supplies. His negative expectation of parents interfered with his ability to take what was offered him by the adoptive parents. Indeed, his maladaptive behaviors from the past continued despite the parents good faith attempts to help. Robert could not accept their outstretched hands. The unconventional strategy was needed to force change. Once Robert, through the change in circumstances, received positive parenting, his need for stealing abated. Correspondingly, his openness to available and reliable parenting increased. Addressing the major goal of containing the acting-out (stealing) ultimately permitted the development of greater trust and mutual acceptance in this adoptive family.

* * * * *

Questions and Answers

1. If the child stops stealing, won't he miss the attention he once secured by means of that misbehavior? Won't he then merely find other ways to secure negative attention?

Certainly some children do find new symptoms to replace those which have been eliminated. However, what we are talking about here is not simply quashing a negative behavior without putting something new and healthier in its place. Our hope for Robert is that he finds healthier ways to get attention. The "stealing game" invented by the adoptive parents provided an alternative way for Robert to get attention. This new game provided an opportunity for Robert to win, no matter what he did. He could no longer be a "loser" because he stole.

2. Stealing is stealing. Doesn't the child need to be educated about appropriate behavior, morals and others' rights?

We make the assumption in the case of Robert that the educative, moralistic approach has already been tried and failed. The real issue here is not stealing, it is how the child uses this behavior in a pathlogical way to meet unrecognized needs.

* * * * *

5 The "Not Now I Have A Headache" Strategy

> **Subject:**
>
> • Oppositional, endlessly argumentative children
>
> **Major Goal:**
>
> • Containing acting-out behavior

This unconventional strategy is directed towards the child who is masterful at nagging, arguing and "not letting well enough alone." This is the youngster who seems programmed to engage in power struggles, to tussle and to verbally harrass and wear down his opponent—often the beleaguered foster or adoptive parent. This child can push the parent to the brink...and right over the edge with his "argue with a fence post" approach. Eventually the incessant quarreling and unrelenting debate wear the parents down to a frazzle. Ultimately with patience worn microscopically thin, the parents' anger towards the child may break to the surface.

The child who argues ceaselessly both brings us close and keeps us distant. He expects and obtains the debate which engages the parent in a familiar, unproductive battle. How can the parent step out of this battle without rejection of the child? One answer is to develop a problem which prevents arguing with the child. This approach was used spontaneously by a foster mother during a family therapy session, when she rubbed her forehead in exasperation and told her argumentative son, "Not now, I have a headache." The therapist asked her to lean back and close her eyes, while other family members continued the session. For a moment this left the problematical, quarreling boy without his favorite partner in arguments. Quickly, conversation was directed to the topic of his birth parents' flagging interest in and committment to him. This topic, the real "headache," was at the core of his deep bitterness.

Before discussing the details of how this strategy is employed, consider the following case of an adopted child with "argument addiction":

*   *   *   *   *

Harvey was an accomplished debater by the age of eleven. A bright, verbally precocious boy, he took delight in arguing any point with anyone. And, he almost always won. His greatest and most enduring debates occurred in the adoptive home, especially with the adoptive mother. This woman, in her best efforts to parent this difficult, abrasive boy, had fallen into the trap of reasoning with him. That is, she felt the need to explain logically her decisions and opinions in a futile attempt to somehow (perhaps magically) convince Harvey that his thinking was awry or that the adult was fair. She frequently tried to "educate" Harvey about her basic fairness, but he was not as interested in learning as she was in teaching. Ultimately she found herself outwitted and worn down by his tireless arguing. In her words, "Harvey would make a great lawyer...he's a real Perry Mason." When Harvey couldn't find a good argument or counter-argument, he would simply resort to asking ceaselessly, "Why?" The adoptive mother, hooked by her compulsion to explain and reason, attempted to answer each question, leaving her exhausted and perplexed. Though Harvey won nearly every battle, he sadly was losing the war— arguing himself right out of his adoptive placement.

*   *   *   *   *

The "sticky" situation described above might be expected to result in a disrupted adoption without some strategy to assist the adoptive parents in disengaging from Harvey. But how can parents do this without rejecting the child or backing down from his challenges to their authority? One strategy focused on disengaging from unbending, destructive power struggles. Referred to as the "Not Now I Have A Headache" strategy, the

Harvey's drawing of a non-existent animal that "ain't afraid of nobody."

approach relies on a "convenient" excuse to avoid an argument, catapaulting the parent out of a fruitless struggle by way of a "therapeutic side-step."

In such excruciating situations (as in the case of Harvey), there is no purpose to continuing the debate. In truth, the objective of the child's unrelenting barrage is not to secure an answer, but to seek a reaction. By means of endless debating, the child simultaneously brings the parent close and yet forces the parent to remain distant. In many cases the child is not content to wear the parent down to the point of caving in. When the parent finally "breaks" and says, for example, "Okay, you can wear your cowboy boots to school," the child responds with, "But, I'll be the only one at school with cowboy boots." In situations like this the child is hooked on arguing and punishing the parent in this eternal debate. This type of lose-lose situation may call for an unconventional strategy, which is described below:

* * * * *

Harvey continued to harangue and debate with his adoptive mother despite her best efforts at reasoning. The mental health worker assessed the situation and prescribed the use of an unconventional strategy, as follows: "When Harvey has had one explanation given to him, that is enough. If he continues to badger and follow after you, withdraw from the struggle. Go to another room. Read a book. Watch TV. Act like you are not interested. When Harvey mutters under his breath, don't let him "hook" you back into explaining yourself, your points, your motives. Don't let him get you on the defensive. If he pursues you, even as you are reading, make a somewhat dramatic and painful report of a headache, and retire to your bedroom. Feigning weakness, all the while you refuse to fight with Harvey, may be the only way."

* * * * *

In due time, the adoptive mother gained a great deal of strength by feigning weakness. She discovered that no matter how strong and enticing Harvey's arguments became, her responses of "weakness" helped her take the upper hand. For one thing she found—to her

"In weakness there is strength."

surprise—that she was much less angry at Harvey, though he became increasingly angry at her. In fact, his argumentation escallated to new heights. The adoptive mother continued to grow stronger by growing weaker. She learned the ironic truism that in weakness there is strength. In a much calmer frame of mind, she could ask him, "Why are you so angry and upset all the time?" Her calmness agitated Harvey, who now felt more in touch with his own anger. He was no longer pushing her hot button, while she had found his.

Harvey had become masterful over the years at provoking others to express the anger that he felt about his early maltreatment. Sadly, he had kept others away from the hurt and unresolved loss beneath his anger. The process went something like this: "You, the parent, will express the anger that I feel about the pain I will not let you see."

When the adoptive mother stepped out of the power struggles, Harvey could no longer successfully evoke anger in her and avoid his pain.

The adoptive mother's posture of weakness crippled Harvey's ability to stimulate anger in her. His "acting-out" was thwarted, leaving him face-to-face with his own pain, as seen in the following excerpt from a family therapy session:

* * * * *

Therapist: *Harvey, you don't look very happy today. What's the problem?*

Harvey (argumentatively): *You are the problem. I don't have any problem.*

Therapist: *I feel okay. But you look upset.*

Harvey (attempting to provoke his adoptive mother): *She has been a real pain. She promised I could go to the movies, but she was lying about it.*

Mother (gently teasing): *Just what was the name of that movie? I've been so forgetful lately.*

Harvey (growing hot under the collar): *You're always forgetting things lately? But you didn't forget what Michael (the birth child) wanted to do!*

Therapist: *Wilma, what do you have to say about this?*

Mother (refusing to be drawn into an argument): *I'm not sure what to say. I certainly hope that I don't treat the others better than Harvey...but how can you be really sure you are treating children equally?*

Harvey (angrier): *You've got to be kidding! How can you not know what I am talking about. You don't listen to what I say. You only listen to Michael—he's your favorite; I'm a nobody.*

Mother (reassuringly): *We both feel like a nobody. You feel you are nobody to me; and I feel that I am nobody to you.*

* * * * *

As seen above, in the therapy session Harvey attempted to blame and provoke—to elicit an argument to cover his deep feeling of unfairness and his abject sense of non-acceptance. When the therapist and mother refused to engage in a power struggle, Harvey was left to face the emptiness. As pathetic as Harvey—"Mr. Nobody"—felt at this moment, his honest admission provided an opening, an opportunity to connect with him.

Remarks

Oftentimes the position which is ostensibly the weakest and most passive is in effect the strongest. Take for example Mahatma Ghandi who through his passive resistance brought foreign rule to its knees. In this case, it was obviously hopeless to play Harvey at his "Ghandi-esque" game. Both adoptive parents had fallen into the grip of the child's negative mental blueprint. Soon came a reenactment of Harvey's earlier, mutually rejecting relationships with caregivers. Early struggles for control in his family of origin provided the backdrop against which all later relationships would be played out.

Harvey, an overanxious/insecure young boy, had developed a lust for power and an addiction to control battles. He was a child who had experienced little control in his chaotic years in a neglectful home. Historically, Harvey's birth parents grossly overlooked his needs when he expressed them in a normal fashion; he was driven to develop flamboyant ways of getting his needs met. Harvey's negative-attention-seeking secured some parental attention but deprived him of warmth, closeness and affection. He had learned to keep others close—at a distance.

The central goal of this unconventional strategy was to disrupt Harvey's habitual use of conflict to distance and control others. This form of verbal acting-out behavior prevented positive encounters from developing within the adoptive placement. The relentless arguing took the focus off Harvey's anger and anguish, while putting caregivers in contact with their own.

* * * * *

Questions and Answers

1. Why wouldn't this strategy of withdrawal by the parent make Harvey feel even worse about himself?

The parent does not reject the child but does withdraw from the battles. Indeed, the parent who is disengaged from constant arguing has more time, energy and opportunity to boost the child's self-esteem.

Could Harvey's arguing worsen or continue? Yes, especially at the beginning. However, arguing by necessity involves at least a two-some. It happens in a "system." Without the parent to uphold his/her end of the argument, there ceases to be a real fight. Without someone to battle, the child has less of an opportunity to externalize his pain and to hide his internal distress. One step removed from the battle, parent figures are able to raise questions about how Harvey really feels. Consequently, they are less the puppet and more the puppeteer.

2. Couldn't Harvey substitute a new symptom to replace arguing?

He certainly could. Whenever we eliminate a maladaptive behavior which served a defensive purpose, we run the risk of a replacement symptom, unless we can introduce new, more positive behaviors. The adoptive mother in the above case decided to tell stories to Harvey at bedtime while he sat quietly and listened. The one rule was that Harvey could not open his mouth during the story-telling. He was to remain silent or the story would end immediately. It allowed a non-threatening, non-argumentative shared time and changed the nature of the caregiver-child interaction from negative power struggle to peaceful coexistence.

3. What is next? After Harvey stops arguing, then what?

Arguing is a form of acting-out which interferes with positive encounters, attachments, trust building, intimacy and the like. Once Harvey stops arguing, we have an opportunity to reach him. What we do next depends upon Harvey's specific needs. For example, Harvey was a master at concealing infantile needs. That is, he had a deep craving for nurturance which he had long-ago learned to disguise from caregivers. His penchant for negative encounters with parents interfered with their ability to recognize the craving. Now liberated from the battle, the adoptive parents could see more clearly. Simultaneously stripped of his battlegear, Harvey was more "approachable."

* * * * *

6 A "Dose of Reality" Strategy

Subject:
- Displacement of anger by the child onto the foster/ adoptive family
- Fantasies of reunion with biological or previous parents
- Idealization of biological parents

Major Goal:
- Containing acting-out

Many foster and adoptive parents have encountered difficulties with children who target them for undeserved anger. These parents become the unfortunate "whipping boys" for children who have a great deal to be angry about. However, much of that anger has virtually little or nothing to do with the foster or adoptive parents. Why then do these new parent figures unwittingly become the scapegoats for the child's anger? Mainly because expressing anger towards surrogate caregivers is safer—both emotionally and physically.

Scapegoating of the surrogate parent is particularly prevalent in foster care where children often misdirect anger derived in relationship to their biological parents, onto the undeserving foster family. If for example, the biological parents show up late for a visit or skip it altogether, the foster family is the likely outlet for the child's disappointment. Many foster parents report to their caseworkers and therapists that the child obstinately denies anger towards his negligent, maltreating birth parents even though these parents fail to visit or visit haphazardly; forget his birthday or Christmas present; make promises they don't keep; make life choices which indicate that their child is not a top priority; and in general neglect to demonstrate a committment to get the child back home. Under these distressing circumstances, foster children—though subconsciously sensing the lack of involvement and dedication from birth parents—displace their inevitable feelings of resentment onto the foster parents. What strategies might help in this situation? Consider the following case:

* * * * *

Matt, an angry twelve-year-old foster boy, had been the least favored, or more accurately the most neglected of seven sons. When the mother was

Matt's drawing of a dragon that's swallowing its own smoke and fire.

hospitalized with a mental illness, the five youngest boys were placed in foster care, while the two oldest children "emancipated." After the mother was discharged from the psychiatric unit, she made regular visits to four of the five sons, while only paying occasional visits to Matt. Specifically, she only visited him on four occasions over a six month span. Sometimes she scheduled and cancelled at the last minute; at other times, she shortened the visit by a half hour. Ultimately she forgot Matt's birthday altogether; when she finally recalled it a week later, she belatedly gave him a second-hand sweatsuit two sizes too large for him.

For his part, Matt never protested his mother's slipshod treatment of him. Nor did he challenge her about missed appointments. What's more, Matt never inquired about when he might be going home to live with her. Similarly, he never seemed frustrated about his mother's tendency to constantly talk about her "favorite" sons during the few visits they had together. To look at his behavior with her, one would suspect no anger at his mother.

By contrast to Matt's "Pollyannish" behavior on visits, he was a "holy terror" in the foster home. Matt threw horrendous temper tantrums following each disappointing visit. He blamed the foster parents for the lack of visits with his mother, claiming that she really wanted to see him more often. Matt "set up" the foster mother to punish him and then railed on and on about her unfairness, her dislike of him and her preferential treatment of her birth children. The foster parents remarked, "Something has to be done about this...he blames us for everything but talks about his mother as if she were some kind of saint...We aren't sure we can reach him or even keep him much longer."

* * * * *

Clearly Matt's displacement of anger onto the foster family stemmed from his inability to voice his anger towards his biological mother. As with many maltreated children, Matt had learned to suppress his anger towards his primary caregivers due to his fear of retaliation or abandonment. While fear of abuse may be strong, the dread surrounding total rejection by the parent is stronger. Specifically, many overanxious/ insecure children beneath it all fear that their hold on the biological parent is tenuous at best. These children are extremely reluctant to challenge the parents' cavalier treatment of them for fear that they will be abandoned once and for all. Thus they "button their lips" around the maltreating parent, while venting their spleen on the foster parents.

In many cases like that of Matt, biological parents offer partial compliance to court-ordered "treatment plans," which are geared towards reuniting the child with his family. In some instances, the partial compliance only serves to prolong the inevitable termination of parental rights. In the meantime—possibly two, three or more years—the foster child remains in "suspended animation." While enraged at his predicament, he often has no other outlet for his overwhelming feelings than the foster home. He continues characteristically to idealize and exonerate the biological parents, while acting-out in the foster home. Furthermore, he denies the reality of abandonment or rejection, though growing increasingly infuriated under the surface.

Returning to the specific case of Matt, the therapist, caseworker and foster parents agreed that a new strategy around visitation was in order, as seen next:

* * * * *

Joint conferences between the therapist, caseworker and foster parents came to the conclusion that Matt should see more of his mother rather than less. Indeed, the caseworker petitioned the Court to induce the

"Separating fact from fiction."

mother to comply with more frequent (and lengthier) visits, though the "treatment team" was not under the illusion that the mother wanted more visits. The strategy was invoked to provide Matt with a "dose of reality"—increased contact with the true source of his anguish and bitter frustration. The therapist and caseworker also stepped up counseling sessions with the child and foster parents. During these sessions they addressed the child's frustrations about the visits directly, encouraging him to verbalize his distress about the mother's lack of interest in him. Matt admitted more freely how he felt: "It seems like she doesn't care if I'm home...She sleeps on the couch all day long." These comments were a starting place: Matt had spoken what had previously been acted out—the sense that his mother truly did not care for him. Now he had begun separating fact from fiction.

* * * * *

If we can help the foster child to deal with painful realities by talking about them, it can result in a decrease in acting-out. The therapist and caseworker should typically take on the role of confronters of reality as a way of sparing the foster parent the additional role of "detractor" of the birth parents. That is, the therapist and caseworker should play "bad cop," allowing the foster parents the role of comforter of the child, when his feelings of pain and anguish emerge. It is important to avoid placing the foster parents in a competitive position *vis a vis* the birth parents.

Remarks

Sometimes children who have been horrendously abused, neglected and exploited hold onto idealized images of the maltreating parents. In some instances, the infrequency of contact between birth parents and their placed children exacerbates the idealization. In absentia the child's recollections of his parents become increasingly Pollyannish. In some instances, increased face-to-face contacts and visitations between the parents and child provides "fodder" for the therapist and caseworker in treatment. Provided with more frequent (and lengthier) visits with his birth parent, the child receives a "dose of reality" which can be useful therapeutically whether the child can be expected ever to return home or not.

Matt, who was an overanxious/insecure boy with tremendous denial and suppression, had long sensed—though at a subliminal level—the lack of committment from his mother. The least favored child, a baby who had been unplanned and unwanted, Matt had denied his mother's unstated rejection. However, his misbehavior in the foster home and at school indicated that her rejection of him impacted him deeply. Unfortunately Matt's continued fantasies about his mother interfered with his ability to accept loving from the foster parents. The use of "a dose of reality" helped him ultimately to protest verbally his mother's mistreatment, which eventually reduced his acting-out.

Questions and Answers

1. Shouldn't the biological parent's visits be curtailed rather than increased, since the behavior problems increased following visits?

In some cases where acting-out is extreme after visits, there is reason to reduce visits. Especially when the child is not acting-out because of denial or suppression, it might be best to reduce the visits lest we jeopardize the stability of placement. We should mention here that acting-out before and after visits is a common, albeit unsettling, problem; and the problem is not handled the same in each case.[5]

2. Isn't it unadvisable to criticize the biological parent in our contacts with the child?

Certainly we advise against general "bad-mouthing" of birth parents in front of the foster or adoptive child. However, what we are attempting in the confrontive sessions with the child is to allow him to vocalize his feelings of grief, rage, depression and frustration which have been suppressed. It is deplorable to perform a "character assassination" of the biological parent, though it is crucial to address reality. We are remiss as therapists and caseworkers if we avoid discussing with the child the realities of his relationship with his biological parents.

3. Why wasn't the biological mother confronted about her lack of contacts and perhaps counseled to relinquish parental rights to her child?

That is often a very necessary component to dealing with reality. The caseworker and therapist should definitely address these issues. In some states relinquishment is addressed in the very first meeting with the birth parent, though other states mandate against broaching the issue so openly at the outset.

4. Is this strategy fitting for use with special needs adoptions?

Sometimes. Although we are not blanketly in favor of "open adoptions," some visitation is advisable in special needs adoptions to reduce acting-out stemming from idealization of the birth parent. We have found a reduction in idealization following contacts with the birth parents. Such contacts can provide reassurance and perspective. Oftentimes it is helpful if the birth parents can remind the child that they relinquished him voluntarily and will not be able to take him back, though they love him. If the birth parents are incapable of cooperating with the treatment team—and might undermine treatment—we may want to avoid arranging follow-up visitations.

* * * * *

7 The "Sargeant Carter Approach"

Subject:

- Non-assertive, passive, submissive children

Major Goals:

- Containing acting-out behaviors
- Increasing verbalization

Those who recall "Sargeant Carter" and his interaction with "Gomer Pyle" in the television series might have an idea of what this particular strategy speaks to. Sargeant Carter exhorted his troops to "speak up" and be heard. "I can't hear you!" was his oft-heard remark.

With the passive/withdrawn or unresponsive child there is a need to help him to "come alive," feel, express himself and be assertive enough to act on needs. There is a certain type of foster or adoptive child (the inadequate/dependent or withdrawn/asocial youngster) who doesn't seem capable of mustering the strength to let you know he is around, or who has found that it is much easier and safer to let others provide for him. One of the crucial elements in the caretaking and therapy of such children is to assist them to "speak up" and to communicate how they feel and how they perceive others and themselves.

Passive/avoidant behavior can reflect and maintain the emotional disturbance of the child and his pathological relationships with others. Wimpy, whiney, "anemic" speech can be used to control others by forcing them to pay close attention, to do things for the helpless child. The foster or adoptive parent finds herself asking endless questions to determine if she is correct in meeting the child's needs. Usually even after questioning, she can't tell. The child's inability or refusal to adequately communicate allows him to remain a non-participant in the family—a mealy-mouthed, avoidant "non-presence" in the home. If the child does not speak up—meaningfully—he cannot have his needs met. The failure to have needs met perpetuates his negative view of himself and—in particular—of caregivers. These "voice-less" children exhaust the family with their passive and unresponsive acceptance, never reacting in a way that shows others that their efforts matter. Consequently the family feels impotent, loses its drive and assumes that perhaps they are the wrong home for the child, as in the following example:

* * * * *

"Jacob. . . seemed almost a human doormat."

Jacob, a pot-bellied, diminutive, nine-year-old seemed almost "a human doormat" to his adoptive family. He was absolutely incapable of an opinion about anything. When dinner was served, he ate it; when the television was on, he watched it. He drove his adoptive parents to the brink of madness—not because he was a bad kid, but because he wasn't a kid at all. The parents were cautiously hopeful after they attended a lecture on "how to speak to a child," but they were soon deflated when they found that their communication was "one-way." The "final straw" occurred when they discovered that Jacob was the on-going victim of methodical, sexual abuse by an older neighbor boy. The adoptive parents felt defeated when Jacob had never once come to them and that he had even denied that anything was happening to him when asked point-blank; their inquiries were met with little more than shoulder shrugs.

In treatment, the psychologist encouraged the family to dispense with fruitless efforts to discover what would get Jacob communicating. All of the unmarked reward charts were removed from the refrigerator

"I can't hear you!"

door and the parents were directed to be less cautious and to play verbal "hard-ball" with him. For example, when asking Jacob a question, they now required him to "speak up." If he responded with his all-too-typical, halting nasal whine, he was now confronted with a raucous, "I can't hear you!"—a la Sargeant Carter—until he responded to their satisfaction. Soon Jacob seemed generally more alert—perhaps a bit "on edge"—and more aware of what was happening around him. Specifically, the parents observed that he began to notice who came into the room, often with a slight twisted smile. Moreover, Jacob gradually started speaking up, and the adoptive mother excitedly professed in a therapy session, "He nearly talked back to me this week!" Over time and with continued use of the "Sargeant Carter Approach," two parents who had caught Jacob's "hopeless/helpless" virus now seemed to be "charged up" themselves.

* * * * *

Certainly "badgering" a child can hardly be expected to yield therapeutic results. But in Jacob's case there was a need for someone to get through to him. Neglected and deprived of affection in his earliest years, he had grown to be a silent, chronically passive boy unable to speak his mind or heart. Jacob derived scant pleasure from his contacts with others, choosing to retreat to his solitary world or to passively accept any morsel of comfort. Jacob learned early in life that nothing could be expected of others. He felt helpless, impotent and without impact. As such, he had not matured, and his passivity and incompetence were more than his several, successive adoptive families could tolerate. His limp, meek interactions within those adoptive homes left them cold, and eventually the adoptive placements failed. The ingredients of maturation, competence and independence were missing for this empty child.

Why is it crucial for the child to speak up, to become aroused, to pay attention and to have an impact? The "artful passivity" that so many children like Jacob use to get through life is maladaptive in the foster and/or adoptive home. Luckily in Jacob's case the adoptive parents had a flair for the dramatic and could be light-hearted. They were able to get this boy to smile and to take pleasure out of his interactions. His new-found assertion began to lead to greater maturity, as he discovered that the squeaky wheel gets the grease.

* * * * *

Remarks

Jacob was a mixed type adopted child whose mealy-mouthed mumblings interfered with incorporation into the family. His early history of abuse and neglect had taught him to avoid meaningful contact and intimacy. In his present home this historic behavior was maladaptive, and the adoptive parents had been unable to convince Jacob to come out of his shell and risk vulnerability. Without any significant encounters with the adoptive parents, Jacob could adhere to his time worn, cynical view of the world and caregivers.

The specific goals of the "Sargeant Carter Approach" were to insist that Jacob assertively vocalize his wants and needs (increasing verbalization), and to decrease his passivity and use of a "helpless" posture in the adoptive family (containing acting-out behavior).

Questions and Answers

1. Couldn't this approach "backfire" and force a child to become even less social?

It could if undertaken with maliciousness or with hidden anger. But, our work with children tells us that one key element that children do read is intention. When the demand on the child to engage, speak up and be a part of the family is done in a forceful, positive fashion, the "message" comes through. Novel and appropriate verbal interventions are often necessary to get a child's attention, and then changing the "unchangeable child" becomes possible.

2. It seems as if you could force a child to become obnoxious by rewarding him for each time he speaks out, no matter how negatively. How would that help him socially?

When you consider that Jacob was not social at all, even obnoxious verbalization is a big improvement. Being obnoxious or irritating to others—especially to parents—is a part of any healthy kid's repertoire—within reason. In particular with the passive/withdrawn foster or adoptive child, we do not want to "put the lid" on his negative talk too quickly. Rather, we want the child to become a participant—in a less disturbed fashion—in his own life. Once the child trusts us enough to "speak up," we can later teach more socially appropriate assertiveness. But you first have to have some outspoken behavior. "Speaking up" is a required first step with these children.

3. Are there other strategies for use with withdrawn, avoidant, inadequate children like Jacob?

Yes there are. The name of the game, though, in this strategy is to convince the child that he can deal with us directly. In some instances merely insisting on proximity—physical closeness—may help. That is, we will not allow the child to become a phantom in our midst. In other cases, foster and adoptive parents have gained ground with withdrawn children by simply insisting on eye contact.

* * * * *

8 The "Mayor Arne Nilsen Rule"

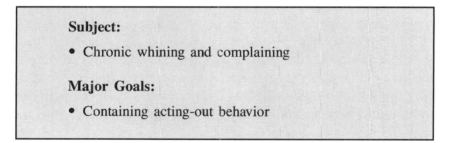

Subject:

• Chronic whining and complaining

Major Goals:

• Containing acting-out behavior

A short time ago there was a "human interest" story in the newspaper about a small town in Norway where the mayor, tired of the sour and complaining attitude of the townspeople, outlawed negative conversation and pessimistic attitudes. Through his actions he hoped that people would feel differently—and more positively—if they would just stop talking about all of the "bad" around them. That is, he expected that citizens would view the glass as "half full" rather than "half empty."

Sometimes with disturbed foster or adoptive children negativity becomes a habit, and the behavior of talking negatively leaves these youngsters mired down, long after their lot in life improves. Frequently this negativity, oppositionality and resistance are ways which children use to either master or avoid dealing with others. For children who have been abused, neglected and exploited, this cynicism is often the "buffer" against involvement and further hurt. This negative, pessimistic style communicates the attitude: "If you expect nothing, you can't be disappointed." Indeed, there is a certain type of child who is so caught up in his own negativity as to be absolutely unreachable, frustrating and incorrigible. Take the following case:

* * * * *

*Erica, a snippy 12-year-old, seemed to live by the rule, "If you don't have something **bad** to say about someone, don't say anything at all." Her vociferous negativity was punctuated by periods of quiet, self-destructive withdrawal. She was a negative "Queen Midas," bringing out the worst in everyone she touched. Her foster parents vacillated from sadness over her continued forlorn protests, to angry and dramatic withdrawal from her when they could no longer tolerate her relentless barrage of "downers." These fine people, burned-out from countless attempts to bring happiness to Erica, finally resorted to the old, "You're going to like it or else" routine.*

* * * * *

This bitter young girl was the product of two negative, combative and argumentative parents. This chronically conflicted couple, blinded by their hatred of one another and their intolerable co-dependency, had brought Erica into the fray as a "sounding board." Erica found herself with tremendous power to control either parent with a whim and to play the game of "let's you and him fight." Unfortunately her own emotional needs were sadly neglected. In reality, the only way Erica could command parental attention was to express a complaint, a grievance or something negative about life, the world and her other parent. Upon her parents' divorce, a horrific custody battle ensued with each parent proceeding to "air the dirty laundry" about the other to Erica. (In the middle of this, no one considered how Erica might feel about the demise of her family.) When the mother left town with a new lover, the father was awarded custody. However, he in turn abandoned Erica. Jilted by both parents, Erica found herself in foster care. As you might expect, she was a not-too-happy child with the foster parents, as seen below:

* * * * *

Erica was addicted to her own negativity. A chronic malcontent, she showed little pleasure or appreciation for anyone's positive efforts. Soon, her foster family found themselves emotionally bankrupt, certain of only one thing—their exasperation with her. In therapy arranged by their caseworker to "save" the placement, the counselor suggested a novel, paradoxical approach which required them to 1) "out-negative" this young girl and to encourage her to complain better, and 2) flood the home with so much negativity (done with tongue-in-cheek) that even Erica would find it too pessimistic. Thinking this absurd but desperate themselves, the foster parents committed to the new approach. Now when Erica complained, they "jumped on the bandwagon." For example, when she spoke of not liking her meal, they complained too, "Where can a guy get a good meal in this town?" And they went on to complain about a host of topics, as they finished dinner. When Erica complained about her clothes, the family agreed with her that nothing she wore looked quite right; then they waxed poetic about how they hated their own clothes, too. They droned on and on about it, and it got to the point where Erica grew reluctant to bring up anything negative. Her remarks seemed to unleash such a "Pandora's box of complaints" from her parents that she became cautious of her cynical attitude. In one particular evening gripe session the foster parents kept Erica up an hour past her bedtime with seemingly endless complaints about the school system and the amount of homework required of children today. The next morning, when the foster mother resumed her complaints about the school system and the unfairness of grading, Erica had reached the point of saturation. In utter frustration she remarked, "You stinkin' people never have anything good to say about anyone..." to which they conceded that perhaps the whole family should be more positive; in the end, they invoked their own version of "The Mayor Arne Nilsen Rule."

* * * * *

When all else fails, sometimes it is better to go around an obstacle rather than through it. Erica was resistant to anything good, or close or positive. She had been successful in turning others off with her endless groaning and moaning, and she had the remarkable ability to play others like "marionettes." When the parents, however, refused to fight with her and instead endorsed her negative view of the world, they "joined" her for the very first time. When they "out-negatived" her, she was forced to resist by "out-positiving" them. In

"The foster parents were encouraging resistance in the right direction."

effect, the foster parents were encouraging resistance in the right direction. In so doing they prompted Erica to see the good, when so much around her had been bad. This joining helped these parents to both see her world and to finally take control and reach her. Erica now less defensive could allow herself to connect, to get support and to feel her loss and pain.

Remarks

Erica was an angry, ambivalent, overanxious/insecure foster child who took control in relationships in an attempt to reduce anxieties over intimacy. She simultaneously wanted closeness and distance; she pulled the foster parents in with one hand, while stiff-arming them with the other.

Erica's relationship to her mercilessly negative, ever-fighting birth parents etched into her mind a cynical expectation of what family relationships meant. Additionally her historic role as an unrelenting killjoy set the stage for Erica's boundless dissatisfaction in foster care.

The goals in our interventions with Erica were to disrupt her negativity (containing acting-out) and to experience win-win and give-and-take relationships in a safe family climate.

* * * * *

Questions and Answers

1. If you stop the child from talking about all of the negative things that have happened to her, aren't you just forcing her to keep it inside?

You would if indeed the child was sharing her hurt and pain with you. There is a difference between merely talking about pain and actually feeling it. In the case of Erica, she did not openly share her hurt as a means to get resolution, comfort and closeness, but as a means of keeping others away and avoiding her feelings. Ironically, disclosure of negative feelings can be used as a "cover-up" against actually experiencing those feelings. Foster and adoptive parents often have to use their "sixth sense" to guide them about whether the child is actually "feeling." Anytime a child is expressing authentic feelings, we do reinforce it and encourage expression.

2. Why focus on superficial changes in behavior when what a child is really needing is to be close to an adult?

With some children, working for immediate emotional closeness can be like "putting the cart before the horse." Troubled children are often highly defended against such intimacy; if we "insist" that they be close, they often have no choice but to "insist" that they be distant. In other words, by pressing for intimacy before the child is ready, we may unwittingly force her to remain even more defended. Such children do not benefit from premature, direct attempts at emotional intimacy. It is necessary in such cases to work towards behavioral change as a precursor to any true emotional involvement.

3. Didn't you mention earlier that "obnoxious" behavior was a sign of health and something which should be fostered?

Yes. We do foster obnoxious behavior and vocalizations in the horrendously repressed, intimidated and meek child (as in the case of Jacob), who has been unable to vocalize his needs, to make demands and to speak his mind. However in Erica's case the obnoxious talk was a smokescreen for how she really felt. In truth, Erica needed nurturance and love but used her negativity as a buffer against the positive influence of others.

4. Are there other strategies that might be helpful for the child who is chronically negative, cynical and complaining?

Yes. Interventions range from behavior modification techniques to role playing. Some parents have employed the use of "time-outs" (a behavioral approach) for the child who reflexively complains. In such cases, the child is sent to the corner each time she falls into the negative pattern. The effect is that the child may learn to inhibit the complaining before it even starts. (Others use reminders or a "silent signal" to the child as a cue to his negative misbehavior.)

Chronic complaining does not emerge from a position of power but rather from a gnawing sense of impotence and bitterness. Approaches which empower the child eventually produce increased optimism and positive encounters.

* * * * *

9 The "Perseverating Penance" Strategy

> **Subject:**
>
> - Children who battle for power and control
> - Children with sleep problems
>
> **Major Goals:**
>
> - Containing acting-out behavior

A commonly reported behavior problem in foster and adoptive children is that of sleep disturbance. While some sleep problems may be related to biochemical irregularities as seen in depression or hyperactivity, others may have an ulterior basis to them. Manipulative children who refuse to go to sleep, wake in the night or arise very early can foil the foster or adoptive parents attempts to correct this behavior. Certainly with some milder sleep difficulties a regimen of snack, warm bath, brushing teeth and bedtime story can lull the child into sleep. However, some sleep disturbances become entrenched patterns and require extraordinary measures, as seen in the following case:

* * * * *

Elizabeth (Liz), the only child of a single, highly religious, adoptive mother, was a nine-year-old "who stuck to you like glue." Her neediness might have been more tolerable to others—to children and adults alike— had she not been so absolutely controlling and demanding. At home Liz would not let her adoptive mother "breathe." Liz' behavior grew so overwhelming that her mother sought advice from the school counselor about her daughter's unrelenting demands. At school, however, the problems were just as exasperating. Liz incessantly targeted other children, following or berating them with a sort of "vicious pleasure."

The noxious problems were not restricted to daytime hours, as Liz loved to go into her mother's bed at night and sleep with her—not just to snuggle, but also to be with someone she could periodically elbow and irritate. Sometime after going to bed, Liz would awaken with a scream, protesting to her mother that she had seen or dreamt of a "devil." Mother, given her staunch religious convictions, would then allow this child into her bedroom. After some months this had become a ritual, and the adoptive mother appeared both frazzled and sleep-deprived.

* * * * *

What can be done with such intractable behaviors that can neither be ignored nor tolerated? Fortunately, it is sometimes possible to transform the behavior which provided rewards to the child into an unpleasant chore. That is, we turn the ideal into an ordeal.

> "We turn the ideal into an ordeal."

From a psychological consultation with the mother, it was clear that her religious beliefs were very important to her and also part of the "ammunition" that Liz was using.[6] For how could the mother refuse to protect her daughter from Satan? The therapist set up this plan with the adoptive mother's consent: when Liz would awaken and want to come into her bedroom, she was to allow her in without question. And, consistent with religious beliefs, she was to read a "prayer" that had been specifically designed for the child. An exerpt follows:

* * * * *

"Heavenly Father, visit Liz at her time of need...and please help her to feel safe on this night. We know that we absolutely must spend every night together lest something terrible happen. Help this child who cannot spend even one night by herself without fear. We know that she is unable to keep herself safe without Your boundless love..."

This "prayer" was very lengthy and methodical—ten pages, single-spaced—and included various ideas incorporated by the mother. A date was set to begin the nightly prayer. On the first night Liz again awakened and went to her mother's bed. However, on this night the mother pulled out the "prayer" and began reading to her. Liz had a startled look on her face but cooperated with her mother at least for a time. After fifteen yawning minutes, however, Liz complained and demanded to go to bed. Her mother refused to let up, stating that prayers must be completed and that it is preferable when prayers are set to memory. Mother and daughter, battling over the issue of staying up later to memorize, settled on only a full reading that night, starting from the beginning. Near the end of the prayer reading, Liz attempted to block out the prayer, putting her pillow over her head. On the second night Liz again had her fears, and was allowed into her mother's bedroom. Immediately the 'prayer vigil" began and stretched on for a full hour, with Liz complaining about the reading and miserable about the memorization work. When Liz would not read, she was read to. Not surprisingly, on the third and following nights, Liz remained in her bedroom all night. As an aside, she also no longer spoke around the house of evil or of "devils."

* * * * *

In this case, when nothing else worked, it was necessary to find a way to turn Liz' "ideal" (getting into bed with her mother) into an "ordeal" and to allow Liz to have what she wanted, but to provide it on other, unbearable terms.

Remarks

Clearly, as one can tell from the case presentation, Liz was a disturbed adoptive child. An overanxious/insecure child with a repertoire of clinging, draining behaviors, Liz distanced people by her "closeness." Her early history revealed that she was an unplanned, unwanted child who had never enjoyed a sense of belonging. In her biological family, she gradually developed manipulative ways of occasionally fulfilling her dependency needs. However, her manipulativeness was only periodically successful in gaining attention from her birth mother. Increasingly, her manipulation and dependency was met with verbal abuse and outright rejection by that mother. In the end, she was totally repulsed by Liz' relentless manipulation and clawing insecurity, and she relinquished parental rights to this child.

In the adoptive home the devilish nightmares were uncanny, effective symptoms, especially in view of the adoptive mother's religious beliefs. They allowed for the repetition of the negative, dependent mother-daughter relationship.

Although successful treatment of Liz' broad psychological problems was not accomplished by means of this "prayerful" strategy, it provided the adoptive mother a sense of competence and also some nights of uninterrupted sleep.

Questions and Answers

1. In your example, is there any significance to the theme of "prayer"?

The significance lies in the fact that prayer was extremely important to the adoptive mother. And, she was empowered by a prayerful strategy she could accept because it was consistent with her beliefs, values and integrity. The "prayer" was prepared with the mother's help and with all due respect for her beliefs.

2. Do other problem behaviors respond to the approach of "turning the ideal into an ordeal?"

Yes. Take for example the young child who was urinating behind the couch—only behind the couch—in his adoptive home. Nothing the parents tried worked. But when the parents put up a sign there which read,

"Nathaniel's Bathroom," placed a bucket there, and exhorted him to urinate there only, it was not long before he was "sneaking" to use the regular bathroom.

3. What if sleep problems persist despite our efforts?

Sometimes this presents a danger to the family, since children stage midnight raids, get into things, set fires, wake other family members and/or escape the house in the middle of the night. Families are not set up like institutions to monitor children throughout the night. Although families can deploy motion detectors or other alarms to alert them to the child's roaming, youngsters who fail to sleep often present a baffling problem for families. It is one problem which can quickly destroy a placement.

4. Given Liz' concerns about Satan, is there any chance that she was ritualistically sexually abused?

In this case, questioning of Liz directly did not reveal any evidence of sexual abuse. Furthermore, there were no symptoms of sexual acting-out which might suggest victimization. Her symptoms and fears seemed more precisely derived from general anxiousness and specific objectives, finding a way to exploit the adoptive mother's "Achilles' Heel."

* * * * *

10 The "Line in the Sand" Approach

Subject:

* Children who push and test parental limits

Major Goals:

* Containing acting-out behavior

We might have just as well called this the "Bottom Line in the Sand" approach, as this strategy addresses the need for foster and adoptive parents to decide how far behavioral acting-out can go and to communicate that to the child. Too frequently parents feel compelled to "hang in there" with children who injure and endanger others, destroy expensive or irreplaceable property and wreck sound marriages. Their committment to the child is conveyed both in what they endure and in their reassuring words to the child, "We will stick by you to the end." Unfortunately, committment and reassurance may only provide the child with a "carte blanche" to act-out at will. The unconditional acceptance may in reality frighten this child, since he is truly intimidated by intimacy and adrift without firm limits. Further, he may surmise that there is no need for him to work at controlling his misbehavior and to fit into family life, as seen in the following case:

* * * * *

When they adopted Willie (age 8), Mr. and Mrs. Blanke felt ready and able for the task. In fact, the success they had enjoyed with several other foster/adoptive children gave them evidence of their ability to reach these troubled kids. Willie was also no stranger to success, only his was "success" at replaying rejection in each of the four homes he had been placed in.

After a brief "honeymoon," Willie revealed the depth of his problems when he deliberately spent Mr. Blanke's cherished collection of rare liberty quarters at the video arcade. In addition, over the course of time Willie began to provoke the other children in the home to rage and riot— against him, each other and the adoptive parents. In general, Willie would do everything he could to "test the limits" (which included fighting with neighborhood children, theft, running away and destroying others' possessions). Despite the escalation of problems, these parents religiously reassured Willie that they would "hang in there with him." However, they were growing perilously close to ending the placement. In fact, the adoptive mother had told the caseworker that she had all but given up on Willie and was losing all motivation to try with him. When Willie assaulted their two-year-old with a series of blows while kneeling on her shoulders (the force of which actually cut through her lips and tongue), he was immediately moved.

* * * * *

Unfortunately, all too many placements of disturbed children result in disruption. Children like Willie seemed pre-programmed for failure, and dedicated to spoil placement after placement. Expecting rejection from "day one," they—sometimes consciously, othertimes subconsciously—work towards hastening the process of failure. These emotional nomads seem poised to pack their tents and migrate across a scorched human desert.

The "Line in the Sand" approach is helpful for the child who chronically "tests the limits." (However, for some of these children the "limits" are discovered too late, as they have pushed their placement past the point of no return. These children have habitually stepped over the line and consequently have jeopardized their placements. By then, the placement is in its "death throes," and oftentimes the adoptive or foster parents are no longer willing to give the child another chance.) If the child has pushed the foster or adoptive parents beyond the limits of what they can accept, the "line in the sand" must often be drawn for the child. He must know that he has a part to play in whether the placement can and will survive. He must be warned of the severity of placement jeopardy, so that he can possibly be a factor in saving his placement. (NOTE: This strategy should only be employed under the most extreme circumstances and, as with all other strategies, with the approval of the treatment team.)

In this approach, it is suggested that the child who is severely escalating be served notice and be provided a clear picture of what is totally unacceptable and what will lead to the loss of the placement. This stark, candid, "tell-it-like-it-is" approach gives the child a chance to apply some of his own effort,

"Taking steps in the right direction."

before it is too late. Given this approach, many children previously unable to break their cycle of acting-out, begin to improve, change and relax. They start taking steps in the right direction. Sometimes it comes to this: the child must know that the placement will be in jeopardy and he may be moved—unless things change for the better...and soon. Without the child's attempts to save the placement, oftentimes our efforts as helping parents and professionals are doomed to failure.

Remarks

Willie's background revealed that he was no stranger to disruption. His social history chronicled a series of separations, losses, rejections and family dislocations. A maltreated child who most closely fit the "mixed type" category, Willie was thoroughly phobic of family intimacy. Eventually, he was placed in a residential, institutional setting for pre-teen boys. As is true of so many "family phobics," Willie did fairly well in the larger, less intimate, setting. Expectedly, with each attempt at discharging him into a family, Willie's behavior regressed and he was returned to the residential program.

Questions and Answers

1. Given a "line in the sand," won't some children deliberately step over that line to see if they will be removed?

Yes, some may. But it should be understood that this strategy is reserved for the eleventh hour of an endangered placement, when a last ditch effort is warranted.

2. Can't this approach throw children into a state of panic over abandonment, as many of them have experienced such losses in their life?

Yes. Again, this approach should not be used indiscriminately or punitively. The child who may need this level of candor, this "reality therapy," is the one who is actively pressing for removal through his misbehavior. With many of these children the "hanging in there" tactic only invites more misbehavior. Our approach provides the child with a choice point and insists that he take responsibility for his actions, before disruption becomes inevitable.

The "Line in the Sand" approach should not be used as an idle threat. The child must know that if the family means anything at all to him, he must help out, gain some control, and work with those who are trying to care for him. To reiterate, this approach should be used only with the sanction of the treatment team and only if it complies with relevant child statutes and regulations.

* * * * *

11 "Feelings 101"

Subject:
* Children who are emotionally uneducated

Major Goals:
* Increasing verbalization
* Containing acting-out behavior

Four brief examples suggest how disturbed children misunderstand, miscommunicate and misuse feelings:

* Jerry, a walking set of contradictions, was (in his foster mother's words) "emotionally retarded." She explained that he would smile more broadly than usual when angry. And when physically hurt, he would

laugh. If sad, Jerry would conceal his feelings behind angry outbursts. Moreover, Jerry seemed almost totally unable to identify, label or verbalize any emotional state whatsoever.

• When Ryan walked into the office, plunked himself down in a comfortable chair and remarked ingratiatingly, "I would like to share some feelings with you," there were a few subtle indicators that this experienced twelve-year-old knew just what he was expected to say.

• So too, when Adrian spoke about drilling holes in his friend's remote-control sailboat, he seemed unaware about the "why" of his behavior, with no sense of guilt, jealousy or resentment.

• Jason, after getting his driver's license, promptly made "figure 8's" on the greens at the new golf course during a midnight cruise. He totally denied any anger towards his father, who spent more time on a golf course than in visiting Jason.

Each of these children experiences difficulty in understanding and acting on feelings, whether from lack of awareness or defensiveness. With some formerly abused and neglected children, much of the work and growth surrounds emotional repair and re-learning. With others it involves learning, in a sense, for the very first time: learning about feelings, what they are, how they arise, in what manner they can be expressed—and to whom. How do we work with the child who has no awareness or understanding of feelings due to early abuse and neglect? Before we look at some ways this can be done, consider the following case:

* * * * *

Donita was a lonely, distant 13-year-old foster child with a "hang-dog" look about her. At first glance, she seemed the epitome of the depressed child. The therapist had found working with her to be a painstaking and frustrating experience, as Donita was so reluctant to share or discuss. In fact, the harder someone tried to connect with her, the more withdrawn she became. In a meeting with Donita and the foster family, the therapist was "getting nowhere fast." The foster parents seemed somewhat vindicated in the fact that Donita was as baffling to the professional as to them. During one poignant session it came out that the girl had "mistakenly" left the gate to the fenced yard ajar (having been reminded of this only minutes earlier), allowing the family dog to escape, only to be hit by a passing car. Confronted by her foster parents in the family session, Donita was totally still and mute. The therapist, mistakenly interpreting her silence to mean "unspoken anguish or terrified reluctance to talk," came to Donita's aide and more gently encouraged the expression of feelings about what she had done. He advised the parents to take a very sensitive, cautious approach with this "emotionally delicate" child. However, one could have picked the therapist's chin up off the floor when Donita, perceptibly peeved by the therapist's kind questions, remarked with some emotion, "Nothing, I felt nothing...It was **their** stupid dog." Hearing this callous remark, the therapist suddenly began to understand how hardened, defensive and unfeeling Donita could be.

* * * * *

One noteworthy symptom of the seriously troubled child is a cockeyed, stunted understanding of feelings. There are myriad reasons why this might be so: the child has had no instructions in or explanation of feelings; the child has not been able to express feelings due to a parent's tremendous anger or self-absorption; or the caretaker has been unable to accurately interpret the child's emotional state due to her own emotional problems. The emotionally "tongue-tied," affectively retarded child often lacks any competence in understanding of emotion. He or she needs a course in *"Feelings 101."*

Admittedly, Donita and children like her have major defects in the ability to empathize with other living beings. Their glaring lack of emotion stems from basic mistrust of the world and years of abusive, neglectful caregiving. Donita will need more than what this single strategy has to offer. However, some foster and adoptive children, aside from their internal wounds, also suffer from a simple lack of exposure to the kind of positive, patient interactions with parents which might educate them about feelings. These children may benefit from exercises having to do with identifying, labeling and feedback about emotions, as seen in the case of "Jerry."

* * * * *

As you might recall, Jerry was described as "emotionally retarded" by his foster parents. He could not come up with words to express his feelings, had little sensitivity to emotions, and his few attempts at expressing emotion left those around him in a state of utter bewilderment. Jerry (age eleven) stated once, while bouncing up and down with a blank expression on his face, "I'm going to kill it and marry it!" No one knew whether he was excited or furious. At another time, when he seemed frustrated he remarked, "Nobody likes a quitter...that's why I like to do it hard." His foster mother surmised that Jerry meant that he was frustrated but refused to give up. In both instances, Jerry and those around him were at a loss to understand clearly what he felt. His expressions were so off-the-wall and primitive that the foster parents felt the need to use educational props: pictures from magazines, modeling of emotional states and practice in the use of correct labels. Specifically, the foster mother posted several pictures (clipped from her magazines) on the refrigerator door. She had written underneath each one the correct name for the feeling depicted: "happy, sad, mad, scared, jealous..." When Jerry struggled to find the correct words, she escorted him to the refrigerator door and had him point to the correct picture. Another approach, devised by the foster father, involved practicing emotional expressions in front of the mirror. Jerry was invited and coached to "make a happy face" or to "make a frown." The foster father would play his part in the game as well, modeling the emotions for Jerry and having him copy the expression—all in front of the mirror. In therapy sessions, the psychotherapist used flash cards to bolster Jerry's knowledge of feeling words, such as: jealous, frustrated, frightened and lonely. In addition, the psychotherapist used a collection of "feelings-in-sequence" cards which showed, in cartoon form, interpersonal situations involving antecedents and consequences of certain feelings. Card A might show two parents leaving the child with a babysitter. Card B followed with the child looking despondent and rejected. And Card C would show the child raiding the refrigerator to "ease his pain." In general, Jerry was saturated with "coursework on emotions."

* * * * *

It is critical to understand the troubled child emotionally. While some children have "counterfeit emotionality," others have no emotional understanding or awareness whatsoever. Very often, treatment focuses either on insight and the "thinking" part of the child's world or on modifying his behavior—

"They need coursework in emotions."

sometimes to the exclusion of his emotional world. It is necessary to help these troubled children make the connection between what they are thinking and what they are feeling and ultimately how this is reflected in their behavior. Among other things, they need "coursework" in emotions.

Remarks

Jerry was a "mixed type" foster child with a poverty of knowledge about the feelings of himself and others. Having been sorely neglected, he had no educative parent figure to interpret the world of feelings. He arrived in foster care "retarded" in his ability to articulate anything of a feeling nature. As a result, the foster parents treated and educated him with the repetitive, simplistic, concrete feedback which one might give to an infant, toddler and preschooler. Along with the general nurturance and safety of the home, this "affective education" provided Jerry with some verbal skills which he had always lacked. As a result, his words began to match his apparent feeling states and those around him seemed less confused by his attempts to express himself and connect with them.

Questions and Answers

1. Are there any other strategies which might be used with children who are so unaware of feelings and how to express them?

Yes. With some children "instant feedback" can be of great assistance. By giving the child direct, clear and instant information about a feeling they are having we help them to "put two-and-two-together." It is up to the adult to sense the feeling, see how the child is affected and bring it to his attention. The healthy and available parent does this unconsciously early in the child's life—education which most disturbed children have missed. In some cases the child must be told, "You probably feel..." or "If it were me, I would feel..." or "At times like this other kids feel..." With the child who is emotionally "tongue-tied," we must often "put words in his mouth" as sensitively yet firmly as possible.

2. Are there any other strategies you might suggest here?

Yes. There are numerous ways to intervene with "affective education." As another example, "innocuous questioning" can be helpful with children who are highly defended against revealing feelings, as well as with children who are emotionally unaware. In this approach the parent or caretaker quite simply points out and questions a behavior and verbalizes a feeling the child might have had prior to the act. For example:

Mother: We were surprised when you suddenly left the dinner table. I wonder if somebody said something that bothered you?

Child: No. I wasn't bothered.

Mother: A lot of times when people bolt like that it's because somebody says something that bothers them.

Child: Dad has a big mouth.

Mother: You're angry at your father?

Child : Yeah, all he ever talks about is what I'm supposed to do around this place. I'm not your slave. . . .

* * * * *

6 Unconventional Strategies for Fostering Negotiation Skills and Promoting Positive Encounters

T he second group of strategies primarily focuses on the other two major goals of treatment: fostering negotiation skills and promoting positive encounters. These strategies aim at developing the child's ability to relate to others and at strengthening his ties to the foster or adoptive family.

Overview of Strategies

Table 6.1 lists nine strategies which focus upon either fostering negotiation skills or promoting positive encounters as primary goals.

Table 6.1   Unconventional Strategies

1. The "Inspector Clousseau" Strategy.
2. The "Wait 'Til Your Dad Gets Home" Strategy.
3. Human Touch.
4. "Kinetic Approaches."
5. Teasing.
6. "Arm's Length Approaches."
7. Therapeutic Holding.
8. "Cultivating Your Own Incompetence."
9. "Shoring Up the Family."

The strategies described next should be developed and outcomes monitored by the treatment team, sensitive to the special needs of the child and family, and in line with statutes and regulations related to child care.

As in the preceding chapter, each strategy will be presented by way of the following: a brief description of the subject or problem area; the major goal(s) addressed by the strategy; an explanation of the strategy by case discussion; remarks about the case and intervention; and a question and answer section.

(Just a short note here before we go onto the next strategies. It is not always the case that goals one and two have been met before we address goals three and four. Realistically, we might be working on all four goals simultaneously.)

1 The "Inspector Clousseau" Strategy

> **Subject:**
>
> • Inert, lifeless children
>
> **Major Goal:**
>
> • Promoting positive encounters

Fans of Peter Sellers in the Pink Panther series remember him as "Inspector Clousseau," the bumbling French detective. Clousseau's assistant/houseboy, Kato, kept his "master's" skills sharp by attacking him without warning as he entered his apartment after a hard day's work. As Clousseau stalked the darkened residence, his body became a "human weapon" as he surveyed each room for the danger he knew was lurking there. And then, the inevitable surpise attack from Kato. A battle royal ensued during which the apartment was left a shambles and Kato subdued...and how does Inspector Clousseau relate to treatment interventions with foster and adoptive children?

"The therapeutic equivalent of shock therapy."

Children who are inert, withdrawn, depressed and/or "wooden" emotionally often require approaches which exceed traditional, verbal treatment. Their inertia, passivity, and lifelessness require the therapeutic equivalent of "shock therapy," not unlike the invigorating "surprise attacks" from Kato. Take the following case:

* * * * *

Frankie, a ten-year-old foster child with a permanent down-in-the-mouth expression, literally never cracked a smile and muttered complaints day and night. Overall, he seemed more like an embittered old man than a fourth grader with his whole life ahead of him.

The foster mother described Frankie as "an emotional drag" on her. He seemed to feel no pleasure and those around him thought of him as a "pain." His constant negative stance kept others away from him physically and emotionally. It was too painful to get close to this child who communicated only through whining, griping and badmouthing. His rare interactions with others culminated in power struggles or low-grade arguments. Strange as it might seem, Frankie took pleasure in lying motionlessly in the family room while others were forced to move around him. The foster family brought Frankie for therapy at the request of the caseworker, who worried about the failing placement. In that regard, the foster parents found this child to be completely unrewarding and obnoxious. Almost apologetically, they acknowledged that it wasn't any one remarkable thing that Frankie did that repulsed them, that is, he was not violent towards the other children or stealing the family blind. It was merely the fact that Frankie was a lump—passive beyond belief.

The mental health therapist agreed with the foster parents that Frankie needed a massive injection of stimulation, humor and nurturance. Accordingly the following plan of action was developed: the foster parents were to initiate "surprise attacks" when Frankie arrived home from school. This preempted his daily litany of complaints about school. In short, the foster mother was to "get the jump" on Frankie, literally. Specifically, she came "from out of nowhere" to rush at Frankie from behind, swooping him up in her arms and hugging him before he knew what hit him. On some occasions, she ran into the room with a squirt gun blazing; at other times she sneaked up behind him and wrestled him gently to the floor where she would sit on top of him. This foster mother became "Ninja Mother," attacking at will when Frankie might least expect it. In response, Frankie was first mildly irritated and attempted to look disinterested. However, the disinterest was hard to maintain with water trickling down his face. When playing opossum with the foster mother did not discourage her, Frankie ultimately attempted to outsmart her. For example, he entered the house by the side door to launch a counterstrike against his mother with his own squirt gun. Much to his chagrin, the foster mother had followed him in the door from a hiding spot outside. As the first jolt of water struck him from behind, he levitated off the floor. The foster mother was surprised by how fast Frankie could run, when under attack. She reported to the therapist after the first week that she had heard what she thought was a belly laugh coming from Frankie—something she had never thought possible.

* * * * *

Children like Frankie are particularly challenging yet unrewarding for foster and adoptive parents. Indeed most inert children give so little that the parents end up recoiling from them. There is virtually nothing such children provide the parent figure in terms of reinforcement. After weeks or months with such non-responsive children, foster or adoptive parents look like "refrigerator parents." That is, they appear cold, removed and uninvolved with the child.

Inert children need a form of emotional resuscitation. Yet those who attempt through usual methods to revive these children often find themselves a little short of breath. The caregiver ends up feeling deflated around this type of child. Children like Frankie are so unresponsive and lifeless that they fail to stimulate others, to invite them in and to encourage relationships. Those who attempt to engage them are rebuffed and unrewarded.

But why is it necessary to use such an unconventional strategy with a child like Frankie? Because without something to enliven and invigorate the child, he remains a poor partner in relationships to family members. The reciprocity necessary for healthy relationship-building is absent, and soon, the parents give up.

Remarks

Frankie was a withdrawn/asocial boy whose incredibly remote interpersonal style left his foster parents out in the cold. His lack of normal human responsiveness discouraged the foster parents from interactions with him. His withdrawal from them stimulated their withdrawal from him. By the time Frankie was brought in for psychotherapy, the foster parents had reduced their interactions with him to the bare minimum. Unwillingly, they had fallen into Frankie's reconstruction of his neglectful, emotionally icy family of origin.

The "Inspector Clousseau" strategy successfully employed elements of surprise, anticipation and play—elements which had been starkly absent in Frankie's emotionally impoverished birth family.

Questions and Answers

1. Isn't it possible by use of this strategy to frighten a withdrawn/asocial child into even deeper isolation from others?

The use of this exact strategy may not be appropriate for every withdrawn or depressed child. However, some form of invigorating, jolting and overstimulating parental behavior can reduce the inertia.

2. Couldn't this strategy be misused by a foster or adoptive parent?

Most strategies described herein could suffer misuse, if the parent has reached a point of terminal frustration and burn-out. Members of the treatment team working closely with the foster or adoptive parents should keep this fact in mind. The state of mind of the parent must be such that he/she can implement the strategy without any trace of abuse or hostility.

3. Can't foster or adoptive parents overlook the fact that the child is withdrawn and ungiving and simply continue to love him until he trusts and reaches out to them?

Some foster or adoptive parents overlook the fact that the child is withdrawn until they reach an almost insurmountable level of discouragement. At that point, it may be too late to invoke strategies which will reverse the damage. Other foster and adoptive parents can continue loving and reaching out to the child without getting anything back. They automatically and perhaps unconsciously refuse to be rejected.

* * * * *

2 The "Wait 'Til Your Dad Gets Home" Strategy

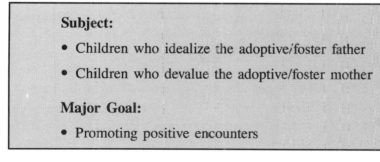

Subject:

- Children who idealize the adoptive/foster father
- Children who devalue the adoptive/foster mother

Major Goal:

- Promoting positive encounters

This strategy speaks to a widespread problem found in many foster and "special needs" adoptive homes namely, that of the mother becoming the "bad parent." Commonly the child becomes engaged in power struggles with her, keeping her locked in a role as the punitive, disciplinarian parent. Over time, she withdraws from the child out of self-protection. This pattern of targeting the adoptive/foster mother is a most common finding and can often split the marital couple, because the foster or adoptive father often remains idealized by the child. The unfortunate child, by idealizing the father and devaluing the mother, deprives himself of a good relationship with the mother figure as in the following case example:

* * * * *

Mother - Bad Thoughts

Father - Good Thoughts

Disturbed foster and adoptive children frequently use splitting as a psychological defense. Typically, the mother figure is viewed as the "bad parent," while the father remains the "good parent."

Splitting

Jack, a slight, dark complexioned, eight-year-old boy from Central America, had been driving his adoptive mother to distraction with his double messages: "1. Love me—2. Leave me." Over a twelve-month period, Mrs. M.—the adoptive mother—had gone from a positive, if somewhat serious-minded individual, to a cynical, cold and punitive woman with very little connection to Jack. In her sessions with the caseworker and therapist, she had little good to say about him. She described Jack as fakey, sneaky and in constant, quiet-but-deadly power struggles with her during the day. By contrast, Mr. M. appeared to see a different side to Jack. In the evenings, he saw him as friendly, playful and cooperative.

On closer inspection it was determined that Mrs. M. was the exclusive disciplinarian in the house. As Mr. M. saw it, it was his "greater tolerance" for Jack which eliminated confrontation or punishment. He implored his wife to relax and take it easy on their adopted son. Her response was stoney silence. In Mrs. M.'s view of the situation, she saw her husband as foisting all of the unpleasant parts of parenting onto her, while he enjoyed a "cozy" relationship to Jack. She seemed galled by it all and yet never resolved this with her husband.

* * * * *

In this case, the family was closer to a disrupted adoption than they imagined. The marriage seemed to flounder; Mrs. M.'s physical health had begun to suffer; and Mr. M. was growing certain that his wife had "flipped out." For his part, Jack maintained a superficially positive attachment to his adoptive father, while his relationship to his adoptive mother was angry and ambivalent. Clearly, professional help was needed, but what could assist the family and Jack?

The strategy employed here consisted of placing Mr. M. in the disciplinarian role. The purpose could be described as extracting the mother from the thankless job of punishing and correcting her adopted son. Her immediate response was to verbalize a sense of relief, though she continued to act in her characteristic role as the disciplinarian parent. At the same time, Mr. M. failed to enthusiastically take on the new, more negative-confrontive parent role. (It is not an easy task to switch roles which have become so habitual.)

"Extracting the mother from the thankless job of punishing and correcting."

After several follow-up sessions with the caseworker and therapist, however, Mr. and Mrs. M. shifted their roles. An immediate and beneficial side-effect of the role change was that Jack could no longer simplistically view his adoptive father as the "all good" parent. Another outgrowth was that Mr. M., who gradually became a target for Jack's resistance and retaliation, began to understand what his wife had been telling him all along. Thus the credibility gap between the married couple was decreased. A third result of this role shift was that Mrs. M. was placed in a position of being able to "relax and enjoy" Jack, as her husband had advised her long before. Relieved of her role as the disciplinarian parent, she could permit the development of a positive relationship or "rapport" with her son.

Remarks

Disturbed children can successfully split the foster or adoptive parent figures and influence the marriage and family in quite divisive and destructive ways. The most common split is of "bad mother-good father." The chasm between parents widens if they have rigid roles. One common pattern, mother as disciplinarian and father as playmate, sets the woman up as an easy target for the disturbed child.

Most histories of disturbed foster and adoptive children are replete with traumatic relationships to past mother figures. In the case of Jack, he had been raised by a "cast of thousands": his birth mother (on and off), two grandmothers, countless "babysitters," and five foster mothers—all before he was placed for adoption. The repeated attachment-and-loss scenarios rendered Jack as distrustful towards, as he was needy of, a mother. He was truly an overanxious/insecure boy with powerfully ambivalent (push-pull, love-hate) feelings towards mother figures.

Questions and Answers

1. By putting the father in the disciplinarian role, don't we set him up to be the "bad parent?"

At first, yes. However, it may be essential to very clearly assign the father this role. The mother, during the day, needs to avoid punishing or confronting the child and setting up rules and regulations. Without a change she cannot take on a more relaxed role, and thus she continues to draw the child's anger onto herself.

2. If the mother is a homemaker and the father is the primary bread-winner, won't she have to take on a disciplinarian role during the daytime hours?

To some degree, yes. However, taking on that role should be the exception to the rule. In working to reverse roles, the mother needs to force herself to not enforce rules, but to wait until her husband can take that on when he gets home. Eventually, there will be a more balanced "sharing" of the role of disciplinarian. When beginning to change, parents may do well to stick to the program in very stark, dramatic ways.

* * * * *

3 Human Touch

> **Subject:**
>
> - Touch-phobic and/or inert children
>
> **Major Goals:**
>
> - Fostering negotiation skills
> - Promoting positive encounters

With many formerly abused and neglected children, verbal or "talking" interventions by themselves are ineffective in addressing serious emotional and behavioral problems. Some troubled children have developed "deafness" to adults and to their words of wisdom, warning and advice. With other children praise, comforting remarks and statements of love and concern go in one ear and out the other. In short, words are not enough to reach these children. To assist them with change, we must first get their attention, as seen in the following case illustration.

* * * * *

Ludwig ("Luddy"), a mother-deaf, overweight, eight-year-old adopted boy with an Alfred Hitchcock profile, had a terrible time getting close to others. This "still-life" of a child had an early introduction to neglect. A thoroughly unwanted, untouched child, his attention from his mother was limited to spankings or other forms of corporal punishment. Prior to his removal from the home, he had alternated from being a "bad boy" who failed to meet his birth mother's innumerable demands, to a "tag-along" who interfered with her time with boyfriends. Over time Luddy developed a "pressure-cooker" demeanor, intermittently explosive and physically aggressive towards other children—and once (and only once) towards his birth mother. After that one altercation with his biological mother, Luddy was voluntarily placed in foster care. His mother quickly relinquished parental rights and refused even to have a "good-bye" interview with Luddy, who quickly moved through a series of foster homes due to his aggressiveness. In these foster homes, he was absolutely resistant to and phobic of touch from adults, and he rejected any efforts to comfort him if injured or upset. Importantly, Luddy seemed to dismiss any attempts by the foster parents to comfort him verbally, refusing to discuss how he felt. Raised as unlikeable, Luddy was effective in playing out his expectations of rejection from others, even after his adoption.

* * * * *

"Let behavior do the talking."

To have an impact on a child like Luddy one must go beyond mere verbalizations. But could physical contact break through to this "untouchable" child? Luddy's obvious tactile defenses would likely thwart attempts to reach him through human contact. Nonetheless, the other treatment team members encouraged the parents to "mix it up" with Luddy emotionally and physically, and to let behavior do the talking.

As luck would have it, Luddy was obsessed with professional wrestling. He knew the names of all the major tag teams and had a list of the "good" and "evil" wrestlers. Luddy could describe some of the most effective holds, body slams and legal "pins." He would stand in front of the television, assuming poses and imitating the moves of his favorite wrestlers. The psychologist on the treatment team presumed that the adoptive father might find some avenue of physical touch in this area of Luddy's life. Carefully, the adoptive father began by asking Luddy to explain the rules of professional wrestling to him. Next, he invited Luddy to show him certain holds. The medium of wrestling somehow made touch more acceptable. Gradually the adoptive father tried some holds on Luddy. Just to be certain that he was doing the hold correctly, he asked Luddy to try to get out of the hold stating, "Show me how 'The Avenger' (Luddy's hero) would escape this hold, Luddy." The child would struggle and squirm free. The adoptive father enthusiastically provided a running commentary, "Oh, Oh! There he goes! The Avenger is breaking free! He is free! He is free! And what will the Avenger do to the Crusher (his arch enemy, played by the adoptive father)? Is the Avenger afraid to pay Crusher back?" In a gently taunting way the adoptive father would invite the fantasy and the wrestling to continue. Luddy found the approach both familiar and non-threatening. As "the Avenger" he could touch, be touched and not feel violated.

Remarks

The foster or adoptive parent can approach a tactilely defensive, hypervigilant child in a variety of ways involving human touch. The parent does this without necessarily attempting to provide hugs, caresses and pats on the back. In some instances touch is first given in the context of roughhousing and wrestling.

"Pretend" wrestling provided Luddy a valuable "emotional buffer" to allow him to take risks. In the context of the timeless battles of "good vs. evil" and "hero vs. villain," Luddy could more safely accept human touch.

Over time these adoptive parents added other novel approaches to resolving problems with Luddy. For his part, Luddy began to show flexibility and—finally—a smile and budding sense of humor. Then, conventional behavioral programs were used to promote more social behaviors.

Questions and Answers

1. Aside from cases of tactile defensiveness, in what other situations would touch be effective?

Touch can be used with inert, inadequate children who need stimulation. Tickling, caressing and hugging can be used to "breathe life into" such children. In addition, with resistant, oppositional children who fail to listen or respond to guidance and directions, a firm grasp of the arm and insistence on eye contact suggests to the child that we mean business. With other children a soft touch on the arm can melt away resistance or fears.

2. Couldn't a physically or sexually abused child misconstrue active physical contact from the adult?

Yes. The act of touching must be used with sensitivity and deftness. For example, while some formerly physically abused children abhor contact, certain sexually abused youngsters become overstimulated by innocuous touch which they eroticize. The foster or adoptive parents and other treatment team members must be alert to how the child interprets and responds to contact. (Note: With certain children touch should only occur with both parents present.)

3. What do we do with children who don't like professional wrestling and who aren't much for physical roughhousing?

How we touch the child must be tailored to his unique needs. With one foster boy, the foster mother found that the most acceptable touch occured while she gave him a shampoo for head lice. The strategy became twice daily shampoos (with a harmless, non-toxic product), which soon included scalp massage. Later the boy accepted a neck rub from the foster mother, in the context of the "luxurious shampooing" he had grown to accept. Interestingly, with his head in the foster mother's hands, this boy began to chatter openly about his day, problems at school and his anxieties about his biological mother.

4. How does this strategy address fostering of negotiation skills?

Children without negotiation skills avoid engaging others. Luddy, prior to the use of this strategy, had no give-and-take encounters with other human beings. He refused to negotiate with others and shunned any human relationship. Based upon his early years of neglect, Luddy was too phobic to deal with others, to express his needs and to vocalize his differences of opinion. The role-taking and pretending involved in this strategy permitted Luddy to be "in-charge" instead of submissive, to be forthright in asking for what he wanted ("Let's wrestle before supper") instead of suffering in silence or blowing sky-high.

* * * * *

4   "Kinetic Approaches"

Subject:

• Inert children

Major Goal:

• Promoting positive encounters.

Kinetic, from the Greek word *kinesis* meaning "movement," calls to mind high school physics and "kinetic energy." From physics we know that "a body in motion tends to stay in motion." But from our work with inert foster and adoptive children, we know that a body at rest stays at rest.

Kinetic approaches are employed with disturbed children who are repressed, suppressed, subdued and unable to overcome the smothering strength of their own inertia and passivity. Commonly, emotionally—and interpersonally—inert children sap the energy from normally enthusiastic foster and adoptive parents, as seen in the following case:

* * * * *

Betty was a ten-year-old adopted child who had been systematically oppressed in the earliest months of her life, and she could not recall such traumatic incidents as her mother slapping her on the mouth as an infant for making unwanted sounds. Betty was raised by the adage, "Children should be seen and not heard." More accurately, Betty was not seen, heard, touched, loved or cared for. In effect, her very soul had been chilled by the icy grasp of neglect and abuse. As the "chilling" had occured before she was two years old, Betty had no conscious recollection of the maltreatment; the impact was extremely debilitating, nonetheless.

Striking about Betty were her "X-ray" eyes, which constantly scanned the environment for danger. Betty never misbehaved, never caused a ruckus, never raised an objection and never asked for anything. At the dinner table for example, she would not ask for seconds, though the other children fought "tooth and tongue" for additional helpings. Most disturbing to the adoptive mother was Betty's meek, unemotional, passive and non-reciprocal style. The other children in the home and on the playground used, exploited and dominated Betty, who would neither stand up for herself nor show any emotional reaction to the wholesale mistreatment. Further, Betty seemed to have no energy whatsoever for human relationships.

Though Betty was a compliant, "low maintenance" child who never acted or spoke obnoxiously to the adoptive parents, her placement in the home was in serious jeopardy. The adoptive mother tearfully depicted the emptiness and lack of fulfillment she felt in trying to parent Betty, commenting, "I'm no closer to her than I was two years ago." She felt that there was nothing real about Betty, adding, "She looks like a child but there is nothing spontaneous, emotional, joyful or child-like about her...she gives nothing and asks for nothing."

* * * * *

The adoptive parents found themselves stuck with Betty in two ways. First, they felt that they were hanging onto the placement out of a sense of joyless obligation and second, they were controlled by her passive withdrawal—unable and unexcited about reaching out to her any longer. Betty was an "as-if" child—a caricature of a child, a hollow mask. The adoptive mother vividly portrayed Betty's total unresponsiveness: "You want to just grab her and shake her to see if there's anyone home...I don't think she even has a pulse, she seems so dead at times...the only time I ever saw a strong reaction from Betty was once—briefly—when a bottle rocket exploded right over her head. She gasped with wide eyes but caught herself and walked off looking like her usual bored self."

Behavioral approaches were initially tried with Betty. The mental health

"Breathing life into the motionless, simulated child."

therapist carefully devised behavior charts for the adoptive parents to put up at home. Betty was to be reinforced for any signs of spontanaeity. The outcome? There was no spontaneous behavior to reinforce. The adoptive parents felt exasperated and defeated and recoiled further from Betty as a result. They had grown tangibly more inert with the passing of each fruitless week. It was obvious to the other treatment team members that special strategies would be needed to overcome the spreading family inertia. They felt that the central goal of such strategies would be breathing life into the motionless, simulated child.

*　*　*　*　*

As Betty shuffled into the therapist's room, she wore her trademark wooden expression. As usual there was no lustre in her eye, no spring in her step. By previous agreement, the therapist and the adoptive mother started in on the "kinetic" exercise. First, the adoptive mother asked Betty to stand next to her, as she explained the fun new game. Betty compliantly stood and listened without apparent curiosity. Then, the adoptive mother bent over and grabbed hold of Betty's ankles as the therapist reached for Betty's wrists. The two of them lifted the child off the ground by her wrists and ankles and held her suspended between them. Betty's face remained impassive—a blank screen. The therapist suggested that they begin the swinging; standing in front of the therapist's overstuffed couch, they swung Betty back and forth in higher and higher arcs. "One...two...and three," the adoptive mother counted out loudly, and on "three" she and the therapist released their grip, sending Betty flying up, across and down onto the couch. Betty bounced safely on the couch, but showed no expression, no reaction. However, she did not resist when the "treatment team" grabbed her wrists and ankles once again. "One...two...three" went the cadence, and Betty made a nice arc towards the couch again, this time with a barely perceptible smirk on her face. As the session continued the arcs grew higher and higher, and the smirk changed into a wide grin. On one particularly high arc, Betty let out a shriek of delight.

*　*　*　*　*

As you might expect, treatment of Betty was not deemed successful on the basis of a few smirks and an occasional shriek. Indeed, treatment had just begun. However, the presence of real emotion in the child created some sense of hope in the adoptive parent—hope that the child could improve and emote and hope that she, as a mother, could have a beneficial impact on this child. After several sessions, Betty hurried to the therapy room and offered her wrists smilingly to her adoptive mother—the first clear sign that Betty was growing more child-like.

Remarks

Without kinetic strategies inert children like Betty often fail to develop reciprocal relationships with caregivers; they fail to initiate, to engage or even to respond to adult attempts to involve them. Their lack of reciprocity—both behavioral and emotional—demoralizes the foster or adoptive parents, who experience the child's "non-response" as punitive, unrewarding and deflating. Resultantly, they withdraw self-protectively from the child, thereby increasing the chasm between them. In the end, there is a stalemate and few, if any, positive encounters between the caregivers and the child. This leaves the placement in ultimate jeopardy.

Questions and Answers

1. Sometimes it seems about the only thing inert children have going for them is being innocuous and non-demanding. Couldn't that be built on or kept as a strength?

One of the central reasons for disruption in "special needs" adoptions is that the child is non-responsive (non-demanding, withdrawn). In our treatment of Betty, overall objectives were to help her to discover her needs and feelings, to mature and to learn to interact with others. "Making her worse" in terms of demandingness and expression of emotion (some of which is negative, of course) allows Betty to develop into a more authentic child, one who interacts with adults in both pleasant and perhaps unpleasant ways. The worst possible outcome in situations like this is for the child to fail to interact or to interact in a totally superficial, unreasonably compliant fashion.

2. What are some of the other approaches that could be used with this type of child?

In this situation, you are limited only by your creativity, given that the approaches are sensitive, well-intended and caring. Some parents have found results with other kinetic activities such as, "Horsey-back" rides, play acting, spills, tosses, games, anything that gets the child moving, emoting and relating to others.

3. Can't we simply wait until the child feels ready to become more interactive and "feisty?"

Yes and no. Yes, we might wait for a brief while; no, if we see no growth after several weeks in placement. Lack of response, when entrenched and pervasive, can spoil the placement. The treatment team can be helpful in determining when to use kinetic strategies and when to wait.

4. What about children who are passive "by nature?"

We need to respect the differences in children's temperaments. However, children who are wooden, unresponsive and flat emotionally should not be passed over. Left in that condition, these children often fail in placements and have to be moved to different families.

5. Couldn't an antidepressant help emotionally flat children become more involved with others?

Yes. Many foster and adoptive children suffer from depression and might respond to antidepressants. We routinely refer children for psychiatric evaluations, if depression is suspected.

6. How does this strategy address the goal of fostering negotiation skills?

Children like Betty were raised to be ''seen and not heard.'' They avoid making clear, direct, forceful demands. Oftentimes, they need to be allowed and even prompted to become more obnoxious, to stand up for themselves and to express their needs, wants and opinions. In some sense, they truly need to become worse to become better—just as Betty needed to become ''hopped up'' as a prerequisite to attempting negotiations.

* * * * *

5 **Teasing**

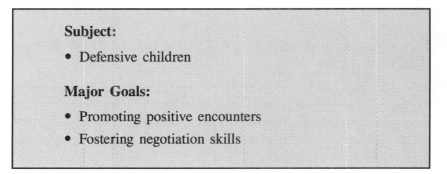

Subject:

• Defensive children

Major Goals:

• Promoting positive encounters
• Fostering negotiation skills

Teasing can be an invaluable tool in reaching disturbed children. It can engage and enliven the flat, depressed and withdrawn child, or it can taunt and provoke the controlled and controlling hostile child to ventilate underlying grief and rage.

One foster family found that their older teen-aged son held the key to enlivening a very unresponsive, eight-year-old "wallflower." Though no one understood why this worked so well, the playful teen would merely say the words, "Is my name Harry?" The eight-year-old would immediately "come unglued," yelling out in protest and chasing the older boy through the house until he would stop repeating the nonsensical question. The foster parents were mystified by the strength of the reaction but liked what came out of it. The little foster boy during those moments of "chasing," was for once alive, focused and—though ostensibly angry—enjoying himself. These parents were also intrigued by how such a simple, seemingly meaningless phrase could cause such an outburst. (As you know, children are masterful at teasing each other with a silly comment or provocative glance, by a brief touch or by some remark which—to the adult world—seems innocuous.) Interestingly, the little foster boy related most closely to the teen-aged son—who incidentally was the only family member who could "get a rise" out of this mostly limp foster child.

Teasing serves the purpose of evoking liveliness and often brings out grief and anger. For example, teasing can be used with the controlling, manipulative child to elicit ventilation of repressed, denied emotion which might otherwise be acted out by the child. A common situation is that of foster or adoptive children who flare up defensively to avoid dealing with issues which trouble them and which, in turn, jeopardize their placement stability. Parents and professionals alike wear "kid gloves" when touching sensitive issues which produce defensive reactions. Over time, these children learn that if they "blow-up", exaggerate a response, or act-out at the right moment, they effectively discourage the adult from raising sensitive points. Characteristically, at home or in treatment, discussions fall short of the underlying pain, grief, anxiety and rage which plague these youngsters. Unresolved issues fester beneath the surface and find expression in a myriad of twisted ways, often through inappropriate behavior, as seen in the following case:

* * * * *

Michael, age 10-going-on-17, was a "loaded gun". His adoptive parents spoke of him walking around the home on-edge, "half-cocked" and ready to explode. Michael would react with wild defensiveness whenever approached by others about what was bothering him. He had at these times a "caged animal" posture—eyes wide open, bulging, ready for any imminent assault.

Michael had lived in the adoptive home for 5 years, direct from a foreign orphanage which had been devoid of love, attention and stimulation. Even after years in a warm and affectionate adoptive home, Michael feared being "dumped"—though he never voiced this fear openly. The passage of time and constant verbal reassurance failed to convince him otherwise. (In fact, Michael would place his hands over his ears whenever the adoptive parents vocalized their undying committment to him.) In school Michael continued to bristle instantaneously at any perceived criticism from others, and he overreacted with profane verbal assaults against staff and students alike—especially when he felt he was treated unfairly. When the school principal announced to the parents that Michael was not "public school material," the family became understandably alarmed.

In his favor Michael had a rapier wit and enjoyed the adoptive mother's sense of humor—at least when he was not enraged. Michael's notable wit and humor, in the end, furnished an avenue for engaging him with some effective strategies.

* * * * *

"Confrontation with a twinkle."

In an adoptive parent support group, those with similarly defensive and disturbed children encouraged the use of a more provocative approach with Michael—one laced with teasing, bantering, joking and confrontation with a twinkle in the eye. Michael's adoptive parents were encouraged to press him to talk about the "ultimate taboo subject," namely his fear of abandonment and corresponding fear of closeness. "Appeal to his sense of wit...Don't allow him to close up on you...Don't let him push you away...Keep coming at him until he says what's been on his mind," were the words of advice from the support group. (Group members felt that Michael had pretty successfully handcuffed the adoptive parents by withdrawal and by explosive outbursts.)

With encouragement of the support group the adoptive parents employed verbally confrontive, playful taunting to elicit from Michael what had been bothering him and to force him to look at how he was undermining his placement. The following dialogue occurred following Michael's suspension from school for "cussing" at a teacher and throwing a "tantrum" when asked to leave the classroom:

* * * * *

Adoptive Mother (noticing Michael placing his hands over his ears):

Here come the ear muffs. Michael's got his ear muffs on. Honey (to her husband) aren't these cute...he can't hear me unless I...take...them...off. . .of...his...ears (as she talks she is prying Michael's hands from his ears).

Michael: *(surprised, miffed, wriggling away half-heartedly): Let go! You can't make me listen!*

Adoptive Mother *(laughing and continuing her efforts): Nope. . .We talk and you listen.*

Michael *(a bit more flustered and indignant): I don't have to listen. I am free to do what I want.*

Adoptive Mother *(firm but somewhat sing-song and exaggerated in her delivery): When a person belongs to our family, they have to listen. You can't shut us out when you're part of this house.*

Michael *(finally dropping his hands from his ears, but truly angry now): I won't listen...I'm not part of this family...I'm going to my room.*

Adoptive Father: *Maybe you don't want to listen to how we love you, because you really don't love us...Maybe you don't really want to live with us...Huh, Michael?*

Michael *(a bit stunned): That's not true...you think you are somebody...I have to do what everyone else wants me to do...Nobody listens to what I say around here...*

Adoptive Mother *(playfully): Huh? Did you say something, Michael?*

Adoptive Father *(wise-cracking with his wife): Did you hear something, honey?*

Adoptive Mother: *I believe Michael said that he'd like to throw the two of us out of this house, for good.*

Michael *(sarcastically): It wouldn't do any good...you'd probably keep coming back anyway.*

Adoptive Father *(genuinely and with conviction): You've got that right, Mike...you can't get rid of us...and we don't want to get rid of you! Don't you get it, Mike? You are stuck with us.*

* * * * *

As this encounter with Michael proceded, the adoptive parents continued to cajole, banter and then mix in a "message" for Michael.

The message was: "We can and will talk about the taboo subject of loss, because you are important to us." The adoptive parents were somewhat surprised by their effectiveness in pressing Michael past his initial resistance. Their own skillful playfulness certainly helped.

"Teasing"—with one part humor and two parts confrontation—sometimes offers an indirect route to the defensive child when direct attempts fail to reach him. As a strategy teasing allows parents to introduce otherwise unpalatable subjects with a "spoonful of sugar." It conveys to the child that subjects will not be avoided and that the parents will not back away from "tough issues." As a side effect, the child receives the message that, though the subject matter may be somewhat "delicate," he himself is not so delicate or emotionally fragile.

Teasing is also a way of intruding, confronting and breaking down barriers, albeit with humor and lightness. This can be effective in assisting children to look at their behavior without immediately bristling. Additionally, if the intention of the "teaser" is positive and caring, it can be a non-threatening way of showing the child that he is valued and loved.

Remarks

Michael was a "prickly," defensive boy—a "mixed type" personality with profound issues surrounding intimacy and trust. His "hot button" was easily set off when he felt criticized, unfairly treated or threatened with potential loss or abandonment. Luckily, Michael's native sense of humor allowed an opening in his otherwise crusty exterior. Teasing by his adoptive parents appeared to lighten communication about the serious, forbidden topic of committment and belongingness. Teasing also permitted the adoptive parents to more boldly encounter Michael, whose past blow-ups had conditioned them to treat him overcautiously.

Questions and Answers

1. If we make light of a child's problems, couldn't he feel that we are criticizing or denigrating him?

This question is well-taken. We certainly do not want the child to take our message as a "put-down" or criticism of him. It is our intention to help the child feel better and relate more closely. Hopefully the child can sense our positive intent via the playfulness with which we use this strategy.

2. If the child does not pick up on the teasing and is really hurt, offended or totally confused by it—what then?

We may need to use a simpler approach...one which relies more on slap-stick, touch, tickling, or general silliness. There are certain children who have little or no sense of humor and fail to resonate to our jocular overtures.

3. How does teasing really help the child relate better and to deal more effectively with others?

It can penetrate or dissolve the defensive walls erected by a rigidly over-sensitive child in a way that is not overwhelming or attacking. The playfulness invites reciprocity—some "feisty" fighting back. It keeps us communicating at some level that we mean no harm, and it often allows us entry into other normally sensitive subject areas. This can be a great improvement over the global avoidance by the child which prevents improvement in relating to and dealing with others.

* * * * *

6 "Arm's Length Approaches"

Subject:
- Children who have problems with "personal space"

Major Goals:
- Fostering negotiation skills
- Promoting positive encounters

Disturbed children often have a distorted sense of personal boundaries and a lack of respect for the boundaries of others. While some troubled youngsters seek closeness in "enmeshed," stifling or demanding ways, others are avoidant, distancing and hypersensitive to even the slightest touch. These children are often unable to find a "comfort zone," vacillating from anxiety over being "too close" to panic over being "too far away." This conflict (and related behavior patterns) interrupts and prevents healthy attachment:

* * * * *

Lowell, a thirteen-year-old foster boy, had no friends other than the many teachers in his school. These teachers—out of earshot—spoke of his "poor, pathetic" situation. Like a character out of a Dickens novel, Lowell had a superficially charming, "street waif" quality. Although many voiced concerns about Lowell and his neediness, sadly his great inner emptiness led them to subtly distance him. This led Lowell to "try harder" and to become more clingy and dependent. One weary teacher described it this way: "Don't make the mistake of showing Lowell any attention or you'll never see the end of it...he is a human leech." At the core, Lowell was the kind of desperate soul who always stood too close, divulged too soon and stayed too long.

In foster placement Lowell was initially met with warmth, love and affection. However, his incessant touching, hugging, "butting in" and whiney demandingness eventually alienated family members. The foster mother, who was the target for much of Lowell's neediness, complained with a tone of desperation, "He hangs on me...He literally steps on my toes all day long...He is like some clinging vine...physically it is exhausting and emotionally it is a 'turn-off'...I just want to get away

Lowell's drawing of a non-existing animal: a three-eyed octopus with sneakers. This creature would silently approach people and wrap them up in his arms.

from him all the time. . . But if I do pull back, he comes on even stronger, makes more demands...He just has his hands all over you—not sexually—more like an octopus." The foster father lamented, "You feel bad for the kid. He's had it rough and so you don't want to push him away...you think, 'Maybe, if I just give him a bit more, he'll finally feel satisfied and act normal.' That never happens though. He keeps coming at you." By contrast to the foster parent's bleak view, Lowell's therapist described him as "a committed, improving, motivated client who seemed to look forward to his weekly individual counseling sessions." Unfortunately, there was no change or improvement in his behavior at home or in school.

* * * * *

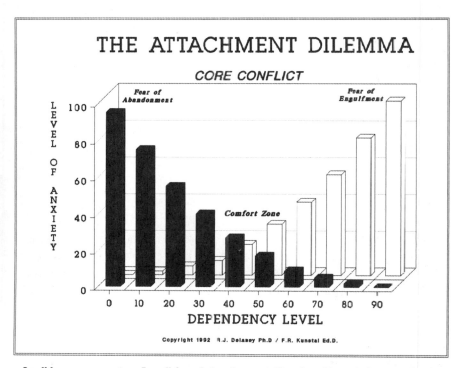

THE ATTACHMENT DILEMMA

CORE CONFLICT

Fear of Abandonment

Fear of Engulfment

Comfort Zone

LEVEL OF ANXIETY

DEPENDENCY LEVEL

Copyright 1992 R.J. Delaney Ph.D / F.R. Kunstal Ed.D.

In all human encounters, Lowell feared abandonment. To reduce his anxieties somewhat he clung to others for dear life, though this only distanced them. Thus, Lowell never secured an interpersonal "comfort zone."

What can be done with a child like this? It is unlikely that psychotherapy could "fill the void" or curtail self-destructive demands for attention at home and school. Lowell loved closeness but expected rejection, and he could figuratively "stick to you like glue." It was clear that he could not be close to others in a healthy fashion, nor could he tolerate any distance or aloneness.

* * * * *

A knowledgeable caseworker "saved the day" for this family by helping them to set up an "Arm's Length Rule" with Lowell. This required Lowell to stay at just that distance when engaging others. At home, if Lowell "stepped on someone's toes," he would be given a brief "time out" in a chair. On the positive side, if he approached others appropriately for attention but did not literally invade their space, they would talk with him briefly. They would point out the fact that he had done a good job. If Lowell reverted to his old behaviors and droned on and on about a subject, he was sent away to "think about it." At school, teachers, janitors, and aides were asked to follow a similar regimen. The overall goal was not to totally isolate this needy boy, but to give him helpful parameters to follow. In effect his neediness had distanced everyone— had put them off. When family and school provided stringent rules, Lowell's behavior became less offensive and encounters with him were more mutually rewarding. Indeed, the structure allayed Lowell's interpersonal anxieties somewhat, though there was the inevitable period of struggling, testing and back-sliding. What had been undertaken was a process of "re-training" Lowell for social contact. Ironically, once Lowell became less clingy, others found themselves with the spontaneous urge to get close to him.

* * * * *

"Helping the child find a comfort zone."

Once progress is made in containing the acting-out, positive encounters are more possible. A positive cycle is set in motion: others become less repulsed by Lowell, they approach Lowell and Lowell's anxieties about isolation reduce, Lowell is less needy and demanding, and others become less repulsed by Lowell—and so forth. In a nutshell, the strategy was successful in helping the child find a comfort zone.

Remarks

Lowell fits somewhere between the overanxious/insecure and the inadequate/dependent type of child, with features of both. His early socialization had been pathological. He had learned to "seize the moment," when a parent was available to him. Raised in neglect, he learned to view affection in a "get it while you can" way. Before his needs for affection and contact could be met in foster care, the behavior that led to his exclusion and rejection by others had to diminish. By erecting observable and "concrete" boundaries for Lowell, he could learn to connect to others without enmeshment. From that point forward he could have his needs met in a healthier fashion.

Questions and Answers

1. These approaches would seem appropriate for many disturbed children. With what other problems would you use them?

Learning of "boundaries" is a critical part of the normal developmental process. Some children—unlike Lowell—stray too far from human contact. These are the children who "disappear," distance themselves, and actively avoid social contact. These youngsters create

138

*massive personal space and must be kept closer, "**within arm's length.**" We have found that with most disturbed children the sense of boundaries has been twisted, distorted or absent. That is, some children are too close while others are too distant. Both have great difficulty in locating an appropriate comfort zone. The following problem children have responded to arm's length approaches:*

— *children who are inappropriately close or intimate due to early sexual abuse*
— *children who are "runners"*
— *children who cannot be left unsupervised due to levels of anger or aggression*
— *children who are at risk to harm themselves and who must be on "suicide watch"*
— *children who resist adult control, avoid contact or who force rejection*

2. Couldn't a child like Lowell mistake our "arm's length" rule as rejecting?

Yes. If the intent is malicious or hostile. However, if done with sensitive firmness, the net effect will be that others are much less rejecting of Lowell.

*   *   *   *   *

7 Therapeutic Holding

Subject:

• Rage-filled children

Major Goals:

• Fostering negotiation skills
• Promoting positive encounters

"Therapeutic holding" includes hugging, embracing, restraining and provocative physical containment. Hugging and embracing, the most benign and loving of these approaches, can be used with children who flee loving touch. Infants, toddlers and preschoolers who run away emotionally or physically from their caregivers, may resist or impede the formation of a bond or attachment. The "hyperactive" child, for instance, may—in his drivenness and agitation—seldom settle into his mother's lap or reciprocate her touch and rarely seek out the comfort of her embrace. (About this type of child one parent stated quite accurately, "a rolling child gathers no attachment.") Whatever the cause, there are many children who need touch desperately but are too active, too withdrawn or too "unattached" to allow, let alone initiate, contact with parent figures. With these youngsters, interventions from parents can range from playful, loving hugs to more forceful, aggressive holding and restraint.

Restraining and provocative physical containment is used in severe cases where maltreated children—massively resistant and guarded—present on-going problems with passive-aggressive behavior, resistance to forming attachments to anyone (biological, foster or adoptive parents), and other extreme, implacable behavior problems. These are children who are excessively non-insightful about their behavior, dangerous to themselves and to others. They are children who fail to respond to conventional therapies and even to the other unconventional approaches outlined in this book. The following case example depicts such a child:

* * * * *

Jay, a dangerous, lurking character, looked like a ten-year-old "Quasimodo". He was not an endearing boy and for the most part had two speeds: brooding uninvolvement and hurtful aggressiveness. Although his behavior had been volatile in a residential center for children, a foster home placement was attempted. In the therapeutic foster home Jay promptly began to do his "dirty work," strong-arming the younger children in the home and threatening and hitting the foster mother when the foster father was at work. He presented as a psychologically and physically "menacing" person in the family.

It is important to note that Jay grew more threatening and angry directly after his visits with the birth father and mother. An observation of those supervised visits revealed that the parents spent the entire time talking with the caseworker, getting the attention they needed. All the while, Jay entertained himself or made unsuccessful bids for their attention.

Interestingly, Jay never protested once in the presence of his parents. An abused child, he had found his mother and father to be frightening in his earlier life. In later therapy sessions Jay recalled a handful of times when he had raised an objection to his parents, only to receive harsh treatment, threats of foster care, and cold rejection. Aside from his fears related to past abuse, Jay sensed that any complaint on his part might jeopardize future contact with his birth parents. At some level he perceived—perhaps accurately—that his parents' nominal investment in him would be withdrawn further if he were to speak up.

140

Behavior modification fell flat with Jay. Punishment from the foster parents only served to provide him with the justification to state (through his misbehavior), "This is totally unfair...I won't comply...you can't make me...Do whatever you want, it'll do you no good." Jay misbehaved in the foster home, as he had no other safe place to do so (except perhaps at school). He could not confront his biological parents about their mistreatment of him and about their overall lack of commitment. To do so would be emotional suicide. All the while Jay was a "powder puff" with his birth parents and a "powder keg" in the therapeutic foster home. To compound the problem geometrically, Jay's biological parents vanished without so much as a "good-bye." Jay was simultaneously devastated and enraged, as seen in escalating behavior problems.

* * * * *

What is the real dilemma in this treatment situation? How could an intervention or strategy here save the placement? Two approaches may be appropriate. One, Jay may need to be encouraged and supported to confront his birth parents—if they returned—about the ravaging abandonment issues. A desirable approach, theoretically speaking.

The other approach involves therapeutic holding which might confront and address Jay's angry feelings in the safety of the foster home setting or therapist's office.

* * * * *

Jay did everything in his power during therapy sessions to avoid his feelings. He would not respond to questioning, confronting, supportive remarks or validation of his feelings. Indeed, he could be the "most passive blob" during these sessions, literally withdrawing into a "mental hibernation" from which the therapist and foster parents could not arouse him. On one occasion he fell asleep during the therapy hour. When the therapist awakened him, Jay erupted, threw a chair and tore up the office. The therapist and foster parents quickly restrained Jay and pinned him to the floor. To do otherwise would have been a disservice to the child who was endangering himself and others with his rampage.

When held in place, Jay became livid and struggled against the adults—to no avail. His rage escalated quickly as he screamed louder and louder at those holding him. He commanded them to let him go, he threatened to turn them into the police, and he claimed that they were breaking his arms. The adults kept Jay in a "therapeutic restraint," nonetheless. While he was in a rage, the therapist began to insert remarks about Jay's feelings towards his birth parents. He interjected questions about the visits, about their past abuse of Jay and about their lack of interest in him. Initially, Jay refused to acknowledge the remarks or answer them and railed on at the foster parents and therapist, demeaning their character, spitting at them and continuing to hurl orders at them— though he was helpless. The holding continued, and the therapist stated that Jay would not be allowed to get up until he gained control of himself. Jay continued to vent his spleen at them. Meanwhile, the therapist reminded the boy about missed or abbreviated, disappointing visits. Ultimately, Jay exploded, "Okay, okay...I hate them! They don't want to see me... They just care about themselves!" The floodgates opened and out poured bile, venom and tears—for a full twenty minutes. Then Jay visibly sagged, sobbed and ceased to struggle against those holding him. Subsequently the foster parents reported that for the next two days Jay was cuddly and receptive and allowed them to hold him as they watched television together. Observing this positive and remarkable response to one episode of therapeutic holding, the treatment team decided to employ that approach whenever Jay's acting-out increased again.

*   *   *   *   *

"Get a grip on the child."

The case of Jay is illustrative of only one form of holding—an extreme case at that.[7] We point this out because it is essential for foster and adoptive parents (and caseworkers and therapists) to be ready for such interventions. Many parents and professionals may find this approach quite overwhelming and intense—even contrary to their beliefs about helping. However for some children in placement, therapeutic holding is imperative to stimulate them to cathart, vent and then sort out what it all means afterwards. Without such extreme intervention, some children may be returned to hospital or residential settings, as their acting-out behavior will eventually undermine the family placement. In instances where the placement is slipping through our fingers, therapeutic holding helps us to get a grip on the child.

In the case of Jay, restraint was virtually inevitable. His explosion in the office—unchecked—could have resulted in a serious injury to himself or others. To not restrain would have bordered on professional negligence. A more serious injury to Jay, emotionally speaking, would have also resulted if this opportunity for venting repressed emotion had been missed. The "verbal eruptions" from non-verbalizing, acting-out children can provide most beneficial encounters with them. Often those encounters follow upon physical restraint. (We would like to caution the reader about the seriousness of restraint and the need for specialized training and supervision in specific holding techniques. Again, restraint is a "last ditch" approach with some severely disturbed children, and the treatment team should plan its use judiciously.)

Remarks

Clearly, Jay was an antisocial boy—a boiling human "pressure cooker." Attachment to his birth parents was ambivalent and angry and set the stage for turmoil in the foster home. Jay displaced the anger which originated from his early abuse and neglect onto his surrogate family. Jay's behavior was so out-of-control (and simultaneously so controlling), that they were unable to reach him at all—to get his attention or to get close to him. The holding approach was indicated in this case, as Jay's misbehavior grew so hazardous that the situation became critical. In the maddening, yet safe, embrace of his restraining foster parents, Jay was freer than he'd ever been to voice unspeakable rage without fear of obliterating others in the process.

Questions and Answers

1. Is it wise and therapeutic to restrain an abused child who has experienced adults as dangerous in the past?

Therapeutic holding, and specifically restraint, must be undertaken only after careful and thorough understanding of the child and what he has been through in his past. This strategy must be undertaken when the treatment team has exhausted less invasive approaches and when the seriousness of the child's behavior, the threat to stability of his placement, and the intransigence of his disturbance warrant it.

2. What about the liability issues involved in restraint and other types of holding?

Foster and adoptive parents are wise to always employ "defensive parenting"—given the nature of the children entrusted to their care— whenever attempting any holding strategies. In addition, parents should be trained or supervised in restraint techniques attempted in the home or office. Moreover, foster parents should confer with their caseworker about the specific state statutes and regulations which govern their conduct with children. It is essential that parents work collaboratively with the treatment team when employing the more controversial holding approaches: restraint or provocation of the child to rage.

For their part, professionals certainly should have prior experience and training in physically intrusive approaches with children before employing restraint or "laying hands upon" foster or adoptive children. We advise professionals to consult their professional insurance carrier and perhaps their attorney about the potential liability issues before employing intrusive/invasive approaches in their practice.

* * * * *

8 "Cultivating Your Own Incompetence"

Subject:
- Building a relationship to the "parentified child."
- Helping a child to be a child

Major Goals:
- Fostering negotiation skills
- Promoting positive encouters

We are often required to change our parenting behavior to reach certain emotionally injured children. This is evident when trying to parent a child who has been raised more as an adult—and sometimes a "parent"—than a child. The parentified child, also known as the parental or pseudo-adult child, has been shaped by life experiences to adopt a role of head of the household. He has been conditioned to take on a precocious level of responsibility as caregiver to siblings and often additionally plays emotional or physical "nursemaid" to one or both parents. The following case describes a "parentified" child who was at odds with the adoptive mother over who would be the parent in the home.

* * * * *

Bobby and Jimmy, ages eleven and four respectively, were siblings adopted by a very competent, energetic single parent, Mrs. Bernard. Six months into the placement, Mrs. Bernard found herself at loggerheads with Bobby, who virulently refused to relinquish his parental control over his younger brother. She depicted the situation, as follows: "Whenever Jimmy is hungry, sick or injured, he goes to Bobby. Bobby talks for him, thinks for him...He is the Mom...They are a family within our family...and I am on the outside looking in." She went on to portray

Bobby's reluctance not only to surrender his role as Jimmy's substitute mother but to accept Mrs. Bernard as his mother: "I tell Bobby to just be a kid for once in his life. I want him to look at me as his mother, but he is fighting me about that all the time. He refuses to be the child and to allow me to be the Mom."

* * * * *

The therapeutic team of caseworker, psychologist and adoptive mother met regularly in "post placement" meetings. The caseworker, who had known Mrs. Bernard socially for years, perceived her to be an extremely talented, intelligent, "take charge" mother who had done a beautiful job raising her two birth children, now grown and gone. However, the caseworker suspected that Mrs. Bernard's competence as a parent might need to be tempered to adapt to the present placement crisis. The caseworker speculated that Bobby, who was raised to be a competent, responsible parental child, would continue to compete with Mrs. Bernard for the role of Mom. Bobby's history underscored the fact that he had cared for his younger sibling and had also watched over his biological mother, who was an often-sick, chronically depressed woman with an episodic drinking problem. Whenever this woman was bedridden, Bobby loyally ministered to her and secondarily watched over his brother. Herein was the source of Bobby's persistent penchant for parenting: his job, his sense of identity, and his reason-for-being were bound up in that parenting role. In truth, his pattern of involvement with others centered on his tending to them, looking after their needs and solving their problems.

* * * * *

Based upon Bobby's historic parental role and the adoptive mother's personal enthusiasm for caretaking, the caseworker predicted that a "clash of competencies" would continue indefinitely without a strategic change. In response, she suggested that Mrs. Bernard "cultivate a certain incompetence" as a parent to allow Bobby "room" to continue his old role, for a while. The logic was that Bobby would not relax his "death grip" on parenting easily and that Mrs. Bernard should not wrest it from him by force. Instead the adoptive mother was encouraged to temporarily permit Bobby to share in the parenting role. She was to encourage and praise Bobby on his care and management of Jimmy. All of this was designed to make the adoptive mother less threatening and to help her to meet Bobby "where he was at."

Mrs. Bernard, although initially skeptical, threw herself into this new role with characteristic vigor. She asked Bobby to perform certain chores and to take on some parental responsibilities that she found to be "too

"Subtly building a spirit of teamwork."

much." He became her "first lieutenant," running to the store for groceries she had "forgotten," putting Jimmy to bed with a story when she felt "exhausted from the day." Mrs. Bernard also proceeded to ask Bobby for advice on Jimmy and his occasional misbehavior. For all of his parental behavior, Bobby was rewarded and praised rather than censured. She discussed his role as a "fine big brother" especially praising him for his handling of Jimmy. Mrs. Bernard let Bobby know what a "big help" he was to her and "how she couldn't do it without him." All the while she was subtly building a spirit of "teamwork," collaboration and togetherness in parenting. This was the precursor to the development of a more traditional, healthy mother-son relationship between herself and Bobby.

*　*　*　*　*

One month after this strategy was in place, Mrs. Bernard reported that the home situation was much improved. "It's a relief," she said. "Bobby is happier and I'm feeling much better about it too...Even Jimmy seems more content...The competition between Bobby and me just isn't there anymore." She went on to state that she already felt closer to Bobby, though she remained somewhat uncomfortable in her role of accepting help and advice from him. Two months into this strategy, Mrs. Bernard reported that Bobby was voluntarily turning over some of his parenting responsibilities to her. It seemed less threatening for Bobby to ask for Mrs. Bernard to help out when he was busy. For her part, Mrs. Bernard reported how rewarding it was that Bobby relied on her to do his job, "I know he trusts me, because he entrusts Jimmy to my care—at least occasionally."

Remarks

The refusal to be parented by a competent, caring foster or adoptive mother or father is a common problem of children in placement. Undoubtedly parentified children—those who have been foisted with adult responsibilities early in their lives—buck hardest against foster or adoptive parents. If there are other siblings, they may also actively or passively reject the proferred hand of the foster or adoptive parent. Staunchly, the sibling group remains an "encapsulated family," a "family within a family." Thereby siblings cling to the past and adhere to their negative mental blueprint of the world, themselves and caregivers.

Though foster and adoptive parents sincerely wish to provide the nurturance and guidance long absent in the child's life, the parentified child rejects their efforts. This child is threatened by the loss of a role which has, historically, given him some sense of meaning, belonging and involvement with others. Though past relationships to adults were topsy-turvy and "role-reversed," and though his relationships to siblings were more parental than peer, they offered solace and a comforting point of reference. This parental role helped the child survive.

Bobby was an overanxious/insecure boy who had never received the benefit of adequate mothering (or fathering). Abandoned by his father and relied on by his mother, Bobby parented himself, his brother and even his mother. Although his emotional and security needs were rarely, if ever, considered, Bobby achieved some modicum of stability in his role-reversed position in the family. He secured some measure of belongingness and reason-for-being by becoming "indispensible" to his mother and younger brother. Eventually Bobby's best efforts failed to prevent his mother's decline into deeper depression and debilitating alcohol abuse. Her consequent suicide was experienced by Bobby as his failure.

Questions and Answers

1. Isn't there a risk through use of this strategy that we might inadvertently perpetuate Bobby's tendency to take on the parent role?

Not really—for two reasons. One, the risk is minimized by the strong mental health of the adoptive mother. That is, she does not derive any innate pleasure from the role of incompetent parent. She "cultivates her own incompetence" temporarily to diminish her threat to Bobby and to permit an alliance to form between them. Once she has connected with him, her availability and reliability as a parent will gradually be viewed by Bobby as reassuring. Secondly, reducing the tug-of-war with Bobby for the job of mothering allows him the opportunity to cease battling for control, while opening up to other possibilities in the new family. When a "tug of war" occurs with disturbed children, it is often most productive to give the child both ends of the rope, figuratively speaking. When we remove ourselves from the struggle, the child can often more effectively wrestle with the issue alone and move in a positive direction towards psychological health and a more normal child's role.

2. Aren't there cases where joint sibling placement should be avoided altogether because of the "sick" interrelationships which exist between the siblings?

Possibly. There is a great deal of controversy regarding the issue of joint sibling placement. Sometimes ties between siblings have been overlooked, as separate placements are made for "convenience sake." At other times helping professionals fail to observe clear evidence that some sibling groups "destroy" placements, one after another. Decisions around whether to place jointly or separately are admittedly complex and should weigh such issues as the quality and intensity of attachments between siblings; the negative and/or destructive behaviors which the children manifest towards each other; and the capacity for available foster or adoptive homes to manage the sibling group successfully.

*   *   *   *   *

9 "Shoring Up the Family"

Subject:

- A focus on the foster/adoptive family (and marriage)

Major Goals:

- Protecting the nuclear family
- Maintaining a therapeutic family environment
- Preventing parent burn-out
- Strengthening the marriage

Although the strategies proposed in these final chapters are all family-based, there are particular efforts that the family—that is, the foster or adoptive parents—can undertake to help preserve the family unit, to strengthen themselves and the marital relationship and, as an off-shoot, to enhance their therapeutic effectiveness. For the foster or adoptive parents faced with the challenge of raising a disturbed child, directing their attention away from the child and onto their marriage and nuclear family is "unconventional" and often little more than an afterthought. Some parents find themselves in a quandry, vacillating between endless efforts in managing and caring for the child (and often with uncertainty about the extent and adequacy of their efforts) and guilt over any morsel of self-indulgence. These gradually overstressed and soon "burned-out" parents can neither efficiently spur change in the child nor accept a respite from him. The pressure to accept, nurture and unconditionally love the child unrealistically coerces foster or adoptive parents into the role of "therapeutic alchemist"—turning "leaden" waifs into "golden" children. With the unabating demands of raising the disturbed child, the lack of support and the tendency to focus on the child (at times to the exclusion of the family and marriage), is it any wonder that many foster and adoptive families look a little peaked and anemic—finding their personal, marital and family needs unrecognized, unattended and unmet?

Fortunately foster or adoptive parents can act to strengthen themselves and family. Without taking action to meet marital and nuclear family needs, the disruptive impact of the disturbed child will increase and the family will lose the capacity to regroup; and as we know, "a house divided cannot stand."

"A house divided cannot stand."

Following are outlined some recommendations to "shore up the family."

Changing Dyads to Triads

As we have discussed, the disturbed child often "splits" the parents and has a very different relationship with each of them. Typically one parent is the undeserving recipient of the child's anger, distrust and disregard, while the other parent is seen as the "good one," or at least viewed in more neutral terms. When one parent is locked into a negative "dyad" (one-to-one relationship) with the child, it is important that the other parent increase involvement, enter the fray and offer not only support, relief and caretaking but also discipline to the child (as in the "Wait 'Til Dad Gets Home" strategy). Since the tendency for the child to blame one parent is so difficult to change, the "fair-haired," idealized parent must become increasingly involved in the "nitty gritty" parts of parenting. Greater involvement in everyday matters with the child often results in a de-mystification of the idealized parent.

Taking One Step Back

Family problems that typically follow the placement of a disturbed child a tendency to increase over time, to pick up speed and to spiral downward. Locked into seemingly unresolveable difficulties and struggles with the child, there is a tendency for families to "tough it out" and to try harder, though their increased efforts do not always produce improvements. There is a need under such circumstances to change perspective, to adopt a "clinical distance" and to attempt to "see the forest through the trees." By "taking one step back"—via brief respite, parent support groups, emotional and physical "refueling" or through family counseling—it is possible to see the "big picture," to shed light on the child-family problems and struggles and to re-think goals and progress in the placement.

Therapeutic Parenting

In many cases, a most workable and realistic role for foster and adoptive parents to play with the disturbed child is that of "therapeutic parent." Too often parents are pressed—by themselves and by outside professionals—to relate to the troubled child with the same care, discipline, love and intimacy as they do with members of their nuclear family (or with children who are less disturbed). Special children with special needs require special parenting. Assuming the role of loving "therapeutic parent" may reduce the tendency for parents to both pressure themselves to "feel loving" towards the child and to expect reciprocal warmth and acceptance from the child. Later, when the child's behavior problems are under some semblance of control, "close feelings" and attachments tend to form in due course.[8]

Accepting Negative Feelings And An "Urge To Reject"

A troubled, formerly maltreated child has the capacity to engender within his new parents negative feelings (anger, distrust and indifference), the strength of which they find unsettling, uncharacteristic and unacceptable. It is important that foster and adoptive parents acknowledge such feelings, and that these emotions be understood as an "occupational hazard" of their special role. By accepting these negative feelings, foster and adoptive parents are able to understand and deal with these emotions and are more able to accept the negative impact of the placement on themselves and family. We find that through the process of appropriately sharing these emotions, understanding and acceptance of the child grows, as do opportunities for change and closeness.

Protecting the Nuclear Family

The entrance of the disturbed, formerly abused child into the home profoundly alters the "family system." While much emphasis is placed on the relationship between parent and child, the other children in the home are also greatly impacted, and their special relationship to parents disrupted. We find that occasional and sensitive "time out" for the nuclear family (spending time together without the placed child), acts as mortar in the reconstruction of their relationship.[9] Careful, strategic, periodic use of respite care may provide the family with a well-deserved "holiday" from the disturbed foster or adoptive child. A common outcome is increased family unity, a reduction in family distress and a beneficial involvement of the other children in the "family project," which foster and adoptive work truly becomes.

Time Out For The Marriage

Key to the health and happiness of foster, adoptive, step, or birth children is the committment, care and nurturance parents have for each other in the marriage. Accustomed to caretaking, focused on the children, and absorbed in the parenting of the disturbed child, some foster and adoptive parents unwittingly neglect themselves and their marriage. Precisely, good parents often take care of themselves last. A focus on the marriage and on committment to one another must be an on-going process. To take time out for the marriage and to enjoy marital assets heightens parental affection and effectiveness, prevents or repairs damage to the relationship, refuels each parent emotionally and prevents burn-out. This re-fueling, strengthening process has a beneficial "trickle down" impact on the children.

Questions and Answers

1. Is it okay for parents to take time away from foster and adoptive children who have had a history of feeling abandoned and rejected?

Yes, but with caution. There are ways to mitigate the effects of brief separations from such "loss sensitive" children. While it is critically important for the parents to get away (for dates or vacations), they must reassure the children of their return and make anxiety-reducing arrangements for alternate care in their absence.

2. How do we both protect the nuclear family and avoid treating the foster or adoptive child as a "second class citizen?"

We in no way suggest that there are "two families under one roof" or that the foster or adoptive child is "second class" offspring. Nor do we live family life in denial of the reality of the child's past and of his other family. The foster or adoptive parents should address the needs of birth children with the arrival of the foster or adopted children. That is, they may allay any anxieties that the birth children have about losing their historic relationship to the parents. Similarly, these parents must convey to the placed child at the deepest levels, the attitude of belongingness, welcome and family membership.

* * * * *

"All who drink this remedy recover in a short time, except those whom it does not help, who all die and have no relief from any other medicine. Therefore it is obvious that it fails only in incurable cases."

Galen

7 | Epilogue

At the risk of rehashing, we would like to reemphasize that effective care and treatment of disturbed foster and adoptive children are based upon a recognition of:

- The troubled child and his "mental blueprint."

- The impact of the seriously troubled youngster on his new family.

- The crucial role of the foster or adoptive family on the treatment team.

- The need to be creative, proactive, and at times unconventional in interventions with disturbed children.

The smattering of strategies described in the last two chapters is by no means an exhaustive listing of interventions for use with "troubled transplants." Our on-going involvement with foster and adoptive families, caseworkers and other therapists produces new or modified strategies to address the challenging problems which continually crop up in placement. Though space does not permit us to present additional strategies at this time, it is hoped that the twenty which were described offer a sample of tactics which have helped other children and families.

No isolated strategy can take the place of the day-to-day, moment-by-moment interactions between a solid, skilled foster or adoptive family and the disturbed child. Moreover, no single intervention substitutes for the corrective, "therapeutic" power of the family. However, certain, planful approaches may add measurably to the effectiveness of the child's placement. Thus, the "unconventional strategies" in this book were designed to disrupt the child's characteristic pattern of relating, to re-draw his mental blueprint, to assist him to open up and become more emotionally available, to help him to relate to and value others in a social and fulfilling way, and to empower the foster or adoptive parents to take charge, sustain, intervene and parent.

As much as we would like to be able to attribute the child's change to a particular strategy or family intervention, we often truly do not know the specific cause of his change. What we can be sure about, however, are the problems, roadblocks, histories and experiences that cannot be easily overcome and that impede the child's healthier growth.

Difficulties can be encountered in using these unconventional strategies, the main difficulty being that, at times, none of these interventions (or any other) works, even with thorough planning and implementation. Six of the factors which might account for unsuccessful outcomes and which impede the unconventional strategies are:

- Serious medical/psychiatric/neurological conditions in the child which exacerbate the effects of past maltreatment.

- Pre-existing psychological or marital problems in the foster or adoptive parents.

- Extrinsic events which negatively impact the foster or adoptive parents' ability to accept or claim the child.

- A poor match or bad chemistry between the child and his foster or adoptive parents.

- Excessive psychopathology in the child directly related to previous maltreatment.

- An extensive history of the child's participation in treatment.

We will address each of these factors in turn.

1. Medical/psychiatric/neurological conditions.

Some children suffer from medical or psychiatric problems which limit their ability to learn, to profit from experience, to understand feelings and to benefit from sensitive human interaction. In foster and adoptive placements there are increasing numbers of children with fetal alcohol syndrome, seizure disorders, brain damage, extreme hyperactivity or attentional deficits and with serious mental illness. Many of these youngsters remain "untreatable" unless also placed on psychotropic medications.

2. Pre-existing psychological problems in the foster or adoptive parents.

The abused and maltreated child is often the master at finding and exploiting the foster or adoptive parents' "Achilles heel." Unless there is good psychological health in these parents accompanied by intactness of the marriage, the child will not feel secure, will not attach in a healthy way and will undermine his placement.

3. Extrinsic events which negatively impact the foster or adoptive parents' ability to accept or claim the child.

Consider the following case:

Glen, an oppositional, immature five-year-old foster/adoptive boy, had tested his new parents (Mr. and Mrs. G.) "to the max" in his first year of placement. A resistant, baby-talking kindergartner, his behaviors communicated his desire to remain young. Along with a number of unsettling behavior problems (such as cruelty to pets, fighting at school and phoniness to the parents) Glen, like Peter Pan, refused to grow up. The therapist, sensing the battle between the foster/adoptive parents desire to push the boy to grow up and Glen's wish to stay small, prescribed "infantalizing" approaches. He pressed the parents to "meet Glen where he is at." While this made sense, Glen's behavior remained oppositional; over time, he seemed to become slightly more obstreperous and difficult to manage.

In talking with the foster/adoptive mother about Glen's lack of progress, it came out that she had been extremely worried (since his initial placement) about whether the court would allow Glen to remain in her home. Mrs. G. was almost continually upset about the indefiniteness of the placement. Glen's birth father—an alcoholic with a history of frequent scrapes with the law—had the financial resources to hire a scrappy attorney who fought successfully to delay the termination of parental rights. A series of hearings about largely irrelevant matters delayed the process of termination, keeping the G. family in limbo. Glen's behavior problems inevitably escalated before each hearing. This bit of information struck the therapist as noteworthy, and he pressed his questioning of Mrs. G. in the following sessions.

After two months of working with the family, the therapist was growing hopeless about the placement. The G.'s consistently reported their growing frustration with Glen, and they considered giving up the fight for him in the courts. Then a surprising—almost instantaneous—change for the better was observed in Glen. He was less resistant, he stopped hitting the other school children, he was no longer cruel to the family pets and he seemed more genuine and loveable. His connection to Mrs. G. seemed to grow overnight. But, why the sudden change? What was going on in Glen or the family to account for this sudden improvement?

Mr. and Mrs. G., following the most recent court hearing with all the maneuvering and delay tactics, had decided that they would get their own attorney and fight for Glen. Despite their difficulties with Glen, they decided to claim him as their own. They had determined that he would leave their home "over their dead bodies." Their joint committment to fighting for Glen "no matter what," comforted and strengthened Mrs. G. Until that pivotal moment, she had held some of herself in reserve emotionally.

We have seen this scenario played out many times. Foster/adoptive ("legal risk") parents are placed in limbo due to legal gyrations which delay freeing the child for adoption. This extrinsic factor may impede the parents' ability to commit to the child, to attach to him and to claim him as their own. Without that committment, attachment and claiming, the child often will not bond to the family. His typically negative behavior represents his response to the parents' internal quandry.

A similar circumstance occurs at times when an "open adoption" is court-ordered. While the intentions of such plans often are to continue a beneficial, controlled access to the birth parent(s), the outcome may be confusion and interference. Adoptive families in such instances sometimes feel as though they "never get off the ground" with the child, never really claim him as a full family member.

4. A poor match or "bad chemistry" between the child and the foster or adoptive parents.

What we are speaking of in this instance is the "goodness of fit" between the child and his foster or adoptive parents. Be it personality, temperament, sex, age, race or appearance, in some cases we find the parents commenting, "We don't quite know what it is, but we just don't fit together." Some children also don't fit with siblings, are disinterested in their activities, and don't share a similar level of excitement, as in the following case:

The members of the Havens family were active outdoor enthusiasts and "sports nuts." The parents first met and began a relationship while each participated on swim teams at the same university. Sensitive, child-oriented and always ripe for a challenge, they made plans to open their home to an older, disadvantaged boy. Quickly they moved through the foster parent orientation and were soon the placement for a formerly abused twelve-year-old boy, Nathaniel. The Havens thought a child his age would be appropriate, and their own young teens, Jonathan and Johannah, shared their excitement. Mr. and Mrs. Havens had never considered that Nathaniel might not "fall in love" with their family.

Immediately after placement, the scene was set for problems in the home. Regardless of their plans, Nathaniel had the same sullen, disinterested response. At the lake he preferred to stay in the motor home and at a sports event he preferred the car. At home Nathaniel's only real enjoyment appeared to be in lounging in front of the television or listening to music alone in his room. He never interacted with the family, and he conveyed by his behavior that he wanted to be "left alone." Regardless, the parents and siblings continued to offer suggestions for involvement, and Nathaniel continued to avoid them or to turn them down. Over time, Nathaniel's methodical pace caught up with them and convinced them to abandon their efforts.

Nathaniel's total uninvolvement and thorough withdrawal seemed to be unalterable personality traits which grated against the foster family at every turn.

Differences between the new parents and child can at times be insurmountable or make it undesirable to try to resolve them. Foster parents who wanted a young child all along might not get past age as an issue; those who wanted a girl might not be fully committed to raising a young boy; and those who initially questioned their committment to a special needs child might have further questions over time.

5. Excessive psychopathology in the child directly related to past maltreatment.

Some children placed with foster or adoptive families have been so injured and damaged by their abusive pasts that they are simply "family phobic." These unfortunate victims are too traumatized, their selfhood annihilated by parents who committed "soul murder" on them. For such children there are so many negative forces and such a pathological history that efforts to correct and to raise them in families are in vain. These children are uncomfortable in, do not desire and are fearful of life in a family. As a result, they defend against any intimacy. They wreck havoc on the most well-intentioned families. While some of these "injured" children may eventually be ready for placement in a family, they need more intensive care first.

6. An extensive history of participation in psychotherapy and in

various therapeutic milieus.

Some children are established veterans of psychotherapy by the time they are placed with a foster or adoptive family. For example, one foster child had 324 documented therapy sessions by the time of his placement at age ten. Such children know well the expectations that are placed on them. They are "therapy-wise," predict interventions, and have learned how and when to display emotions. They very quickly have the therapist "on the ropes."

Final Remarks

Throughout this book we have stressed the essential participation of foster or adoptive families in the child's treatment.[10] We proposed an alternative to traditional family systems thinking—particularly as this applies to cases of foster or adoptive placement of the seriously disturbed child. Given our family perspective, the following factors increase the odds of reaching the child and helping the placement:

- The therapist views his relationship to the child as secondary to the child's relationships to members of his foster or adoptive family.

- Interventions and therapy are family-based.

- The family is incorporated as part of a "therapeutic team."

- The foster or adoptive parents attend to their own individual and marital health and have the ability and skills to be open, creative, "risk taking" and novel in their approaches to helping the troubled child.

Unfortunately, there are many cases where the child's individual therapy is seen by the therapist as positive, impactful, growth-promoting and remediative—while the child's family (foster or adoptive) is falling apart. Under these dire circumstances, we often find that *"psychotherapy was a success, but the placement died."* However, when helping professionals work together with foster or adoptive parents as part of a "treatment team," there is a positive impact on the family and a heightened ability to reach "troubled transplants."

REFERENCES

Ainsworth, Mary D. Salter; Blehar, Mary; Waters, Everett; and Wall, Sally. *Patterns of Attachment: A Psychological Study of the Strange Situation*. New Jersey: Lawrence Erlbaum Associates, 1978.

Anthony, E. James and Cohler, Bertram, J. (Eds.) *The Invulnerable Child*. New York: Guilford Press, 1987.

Barkley, Russell. *Attention-Deficit Hyperactivity Disorder: A Handbook for Diagnosis and Treatment*. New York: Guilford Press. 1990

Barrnett, R. Joffree, Docherty, John, and Frommelt, Gayle. "A Review of Child Psychotherapy Research Since 1963," In *Journal of the American Academy of Child and Adolescent Psychiatry*, Vol 30, No. 1, January, 1991.

Bates, John and Bayles, Kathryn. "Attachment and the Development of Behavior Problems," In Jay Belsky and Teresa Nezworski (Eds.) *Clinical Implications of Attachment*. New Jersey: Lawrence Erlbaum Associates, 1988.

Belsky, Jay and Nezworski, Teresa. *Clinical Implications of Attachment*. New Jersey: Lawrence Erlbaum Associates, 1988.

Bowlby, John. *Attachment and Loss. Volume I: Attachment*. New York: Basic Books, 1969.

Bowlby, John. *Attachment and Loss. Volume II: Separation*. New York: Basic Books, 1973.

Brazelton, T. Berry and Cramer, Bertrand G. *The Earliest Relationship*. New York: Addison-Wesley Publishing, 1990.

Bretherton, Inge; Ridgeway, Doreen; and Cassidy, Jude. "Assessing Internal Working Models of the Attachment Relationship: An Attachment Story Completion Task for Three-Year-Olds." In Mark T. Greenberg; Dante Cicchetti; and E. Mark Cummings (Eds.), *Attachment in the Preschool Years*. Chicago: University of Chicago Press, 1990.

Cline, Foster. *Understanding and Treating the Severely Disturbed Child*. Evergreen, CO: Evergreen Consultants, 1979.

Coleman, Loren; Tilbor, Karen; Hornby, Helaine; and Boggis, Carol. *Working with Older Adoptees*. Portland, ME: University of Southern Maine, 1988.

Delaney, Richard. *Attachment Problems in Children*. Unpublished manuscript. 1991.

Delaney, Richard. *Fostering Changes: Treating Attachment-Disordered Foster Children*. Ft. Collins, CO: Walter J. Corbett, 1991.

DiLeo, Joseph. *Children's Drawings As Diagnostic Aids*. New York: Brunner/Mazel, 1973.

Dollard, John and Miller, Neal. *Personality and Psychotherapy.* New York: McGraw-Hill, 1950.

Dorris, Michael. *The Broken Cord.* New York: Harper Perennial, 1989.

Dreikurs, Rudolf. *Children the Challenge.* New York: Hawthorne, 1964.

Fahlberg, Vera. *A Child's Journey Through Placement.* Indianapolis, IN: Perspectives Press, 1991.

Fahlberg, Vera Colburn. *Attachment and Separation.* Lansing, Michigan: Office of Family and Youth Services, 1979.

Fraiberg, Selma. *Clinical Studies in Infant Mental Health.* New York: Basic Books, 1980.

Grabe, Pam (Editor). *Adoption Resources for Mental Health Professionals.* Mercer, PA: Mental Health Adoption Therapy Project, 1986.

Greenberg, Mark T.; Cicchetti; Dante; and Cummings, E. Mark (Eds). *Attachment in the Preschool Years.* Chicago: University of Chicago Press, 1990.

Group for the Advancement of Psychiatry. *Psychological Disorders in Childhood.* New York: GAP, 1966.

Hunt, J. McVicker. *Intelligence and Experience.* New York: Ronald Press, 1961.

Jones, Barbara McComb; Jenstrom, Linda; and MacFarlane, Kee. *Sexual Abuse of Children: Selected Readings.* National Center on Child Abuse and Neglect. DHHS Publication No. 78-30161, 1980.

Kagan, Jerome. *The Nature of the Child.* New York: Basic Books, 1984.

Kashani, Javad; Daniel, Anasseril; Dandoy, Alison; and Holcomb, William. "Family Violence: Impact on Children," *Journal of Child and Adolescent Psychiatry.* Volume 31, Number 2, March, 1992.

Katz, Linda and Robinson, Chris. "Foster Care Drift: A Risk-Assessment Matrix," *Child Welfare,* Volume LXX, Number 3, May-June, 1991.

Katz, Linda. "An Overview of Current Clinical Issues in Separation and Placement," *Child and Adolescent Social Work,* Human Sciences Press, 1985.

Krill, Don. Personal communication with the author. 1992

Lieberman, Alicia and Pawl, Jaree. "Clinical Applications of Attachment Theory," In Jay Belsky and Teresa Nezworski (Eds.) *Clinical Implications of Attachment.* New Jersey: Lawrence Erlbaum Associates, 1988.

Madanes, Cloe. *Behind the One-Way Mirror: Advances in the Practice of Strategic Therapy.* San Francisco: Jossey Bass, 1986.

Magid, Ken and McKelvey, Carole. *High Risk: Children Without A Conscience.* New York: Bantam Books, 1987

Mahler, Margaret; Pine, Fred; and Bergman, Anni. *The Psychological*

Birth of the Human Infant. New York: Basic Books, 1975.

Main, Mary and Solomon, Judith. "Procedures for Identifying Infants as Disorganized/Disoriented During the Ainsworth Strange Situation," In Mark T. Greenberg; Dante Cicchetti; and E. Mark Cummings (Eds.), *Attachment in the Preschool Years*. Chicago: University of Chicago Press, 1990.

Main, Mary and Hesse, Erik. "Parents' Unresolved Traumatic Experiences Are Related to Infant Disorganize Attachment Status: Is Frightened and/or Frightening Parental Behavior the Linking Mechanism?" In Mark T. Greenberg; Dante Cicchetti; and E. Mark Cummings (Eds.) *Attachment in the Preschool Years*. Chicago: University of Chicago Press, 1990.

Masterson, James. *Treatment of the Borderline Adolescent*. New York: Wiley-Interscience, 1972.

McDermott, John; Fraiberg, Selma; and Harrison, Saul I. "Residential Treatment of Children: The Utilization of Transference Behavior," in Stella Chess and Alexander Thomas (Eds.) *Annual Progress in Child Psychiatry and Child Development*. New York: Brunner/Mazel, 1969.

Minuchin, Salvador. *Families and Family Therapy*. Cambridge: Harvard University Press, 1974.

Mrazek, Patricia Beezley and Kempe, C. Henry (Editors). *Sexually Abused Children and their Families*. New York: Pergamon Press, 1981.

Napier, Augustus and Whitaker, Carl. *The Family Crucible*. New York: Harper and Row, 1978.

Pearson, Gerald. *A Handbook of Child Psychoanalysis*. New York: Basic Books, 1968.

Partridge, Susan; Hornby, Helaine; and McDonald, Thomas. *Legacies of Loss: Visions of Gain*. Washington, D.C. USDHHS (OHD), 1986.

Partridge, Susan; Hornby, Helaine; and McDonald, Thomas. *Learning from Adoption Disruption: Insights from Practice*. Portland, ME: Human Services Development, 1986.

Pound, Andrea. "Attachment and Maternal Depression," In Colin Murray Parkes and Joan Stevenson-Hinde (Eds.), *Attachment in Human Behavior*. New York: Basic Books, 1982.

Pytkowicz Streissguth, Ann. and Giunta, Carole. "Mental Health and Health Needs of Infants and Preschool Children with Fetal Alcohol Syndrome," *International Journal of Family Psychiatry*, Vol 9, No. 1, 29-47, 1988.

Robertson, James and Robertson, Joyce. *Separation and the Very Young*. London: Free Association Books, 1989.

Schneider-Rosen, Karen. "The Develomental Reorganization of Attachment Relationships: Guidelines for Classification Beyond

Infancy," In Mark T. Greenberg; Dante Cicchetti; and E. Mark
Cummings (Eds.), *Attachment in the Preschool Years.* Chicago:
University of Chicago Press, 1990.

Schwartz, Richard. "Beyond Essentialism," *The Family Therapy
Networker,* January-February, 1992.

Speltz, Matthew. "The Treatment of Preschool Conduct Problems: An
Integration of Behavioral and Attachment Concepts," In Mark T.
Greenberg; Dante Cicchetti; and E. Mark Cummings (Eds.),
Attachment in the Preschool Years. Chicago: University of Chicago
Press, 1990.

Spieker, Susan and Booth, Cathryn. "Maternal Antecedents of
Attachment Quality," In Jay Belsky and Teresa Nezworski (Eds.)
Clinical Implications of Attachment. New Jersey: Lawrence Erlbaum
Associates, 1988.

Stroufe, L. Alan. "The Role of Infant-Caregiver Attachment in
Development," In Jay Belsky and Teresa Nezworski (Eds.) *Clinical
Implications of Attachment.* New Jersey: Lawrence Erlbaum
Associates, 1988.

Welch, Martha. *Holding Time.* New York: Simon and Schuster, 1988.

Whitaker, Carl and Bumberry, William. *Dancing with the Family.* New
York: Brunner Mazel, 1988.

Wiltse, Kermit T. "Foster Care—An Overview," In Joan Laird and Ann
Hartman (Eds.), *A Handbook of Child Welfare.* New York: The Free
Press, 1985.

Related Publications

Anne Anastasi. *Psychological Testing.* New York: MacMillan Publishing,
1968.

Cicchetti, Dante; Cummings, E. Mark; Greenberg, Mark T.; and
Marvin, Robert S. "An Organizational Perspective on Attachment
Beyond Infancy: Implications for Theory, Measurement, and
Research," In Mark T. Greenberg; Dante Cicchetti; and E. Mark
Cummings (Eds.), *Attachment in the Preschool Years.* Chicago:
University of Chicago Press, 1990.

Crittenden, Patricia. "Relationships at Risk," In Jay Belsky and Teresa
Nezworski (Eds.) *Clinical Implications of Attachment.* New Jersey:
Lawrence Erlbaum Associates, 1988.

Diagnostic and Statistics Manual III-Revised. Washington, D.C.:
American Psychiatric Association, 1987.

Erikson, Erik H. *Childhood and Society.* New York: Norton, 1963.

Fanshel, David. "Status Changes of Children in Foster Care," In Stella Chess and Alexander Thomas (Eds.), *Annual Progress in Child Psychiatry and Child Development,* 1977.

Goldstein, Joseph; Freud, Anna; and Solnit, Albert J. *Beyond the Best Interests of the Child.* New York: Free Press, 1973.

Greenberg, Mark and Speltz, Matthew. "Attachment and the Ontogeny of Conduct Problems," In Jay Belsky and Teresa Nezworksi (Eds.) *Clinical Implications of Attachment.* New Jersey: Lawrence Erlbaum Associates, 1988.

Greenspan, Stanley I. and Lieberman, Alicia F. "A Clinical Approach to Attachment," In Jay Belsky and Teresa Nezworski (Eds.) *Clinical Implications of Attachment.* New Jersey: Lawrence Erlbaum Associates, 1988.

Haley, Jay. *Uncommon Therapy.* New York: W.W. Norton and Company, 1973.

Jewett, Claudia. *Adopting the Older Child.* Boston: The Harvard Common Press, 1978.

Kempe, C. Henry and Helfer, Ray E. *Helping the Battered Child and His Family.* Philadelphia: Lippincott, 1972.

Minuchin, Salvador. *Families and Family Therapy.* Cambridge: Harvard University Press, 1974.

Minuchin, Salvador and Fishman, H. Charles. *Family Therapy Techniques.* Massachusettes: Harvard University Press, 1981.

Palazzoli, M.S., Boscolo, L., Cecchin, G., and Prata, G. *Paradox and Counterparadox.* New Jersey: Jason Aronson, 1990.

Parkes, Colin Murray and Stevenson-Hinde, Joan (Eds.). *The Place of Attachment in Human Behavior.* New York: Basic Books, 1982.

Redl, Fritz and Wineman, David. *Children Who Hate.* New York: Free Press, 1951.

Rose, Thomas and Rose, Dorothea Wend. "Adoption, Foster Care, and Group Homes for Handicapped Children," In Ann Hartman and Joan Laird (Eds.), *A Handbook of Child Welfare.* New York: Free Press, 1985.

Rosen, Sidney. *My Voice Will Go With You.* New York: W.W. Norton and Company, 1982.

Sameroff, Arnold and Emde, Robert. *Relationship Disturbance in Early Childhood.* New York: Basic Books, 1989.

Siegel, Barry. *A Death in White Bear Lake.* New York: Bantam Books, 1990.

Sperling, Melitta. *The Major Neuroses and Behavior Disorders in Children.* New York: Aronson, 1974.

Spitz, Rene. *The First Year of Life.* New York: International Universities

Press, 1965.

Swire, Margaret and Kavaler, Florence. "The Health Status of Foster Children," *Child Welfare,* Volume 56, 635-653, 1977.

Whitaker, Carl. *Midnight Musings of A Family Therapist.* New York: W.W. Norton, 1989.

Whittaker, James T. "Group and Institutional Care—An Overview," In Ann Hartman and Joan Laird (Eds.), *A Handbook of Child Welfare.* New York: Free Press, 1985.

Woolf, Gaetana DiBerto. "An Outlook for Foster Care in the United States," *Child Welfare,* Volume LXIX, No. 1, Jan/Feb, 1990.

FOOTNOTES

[1] The five categories described herein cannot depict the disturbed foster or adoptive child completely. The reader is referred to the *Diagnostic and Statistical Manual of Mental Disorders (DSM III-R)* for the most comprehensive classification of emotional and behavioral disorders in children (and adults), including such conditions as: mental retardation, seizure disorders, pervasive developmental disorders, schizophrenia, separation anxiety, and oppositional-defiant disorder.

[2] Working with biological parents is often of vital importance to the foster or adoptive child. A thorough discussion of direct involvement with birth parents is beyond the scope or intent of this book. Please see Vera Fahlberg's *A Child's Journey Through Placement* for a sensitive presentation on birth parent involvement. It should be mentioned here that in many cases in foster care, family preservation should be of central concern to those working with the child and his biological relatives.

[3] Note: We would caution the reader against using the withdrawal of nourishing food from children. Additionally, children with eating disorders may require thorough medical/psychiatric evaluations focused upon possible physical causes and effects. Bulimia, anorexia and clinical depression are often correlated with certain eating disorders in disturbed children.

[4] Note: We advise emphatically against the use of threats of abandonment with children. Further, the therapeutic team must scrupulously avoid humiliating or denigrating the child with any strategies they employ. In all cases, strategies must be devoid of any hosility or insensitivity to the child. Lastly, children who frequently become tearful, moody, volatile, or labile emotionally and who demonstrate such vegetative symptoms as sleep or eating problems, may suffer from clinical depression. In such cases, depression and suicidality should be evaluated by the mental health professionals on the treatment team.

[5] Visitation must comply, of course, with relevant court-ordered treatment plans which address the issue of parent-child contacts. When ultimate reunion of birth parents and child(ren) is the stated or legislated goal of placement and interventions, this may impact the strategies designed for the child.

6   The use of "theological interventions" with a child should abide by pertinent state regulations and should be respectful to the religious beliefs of the parent figures and the child.

7   How holding is specifically employed with children depends upon such factors as the child's needs, physical health, age, sex, history of abuse, and past and current response to holding approaches. Holding and cuddling may be contraindicated, for example, for a formerly sexually abused teen-aged girl, while it may be "just what the doctor ordered" for an unresponsive infant with a diagnosis of failure-to-thrive. Additionally, the more intrusive, restraining and provocative holding strategy used, the more close monitoring by the treatment team is required.

8   In no way do we wish to imply that foster or adoptive parents should be aloof, uncaring, or uninvolved with their children, nor should they meet parenting responsibilities in a cavalier, uncommitted fashion. What we address here is the need for their parents to divest themselves of any unrealistic, counterproductive pressures to attach and love prematurely.

9   Note: Foster and adoptive parents are strongly advised against using strategies which send a message to the child that he is a "second class" family member. However, empathic concern for nuclear family members and for any adjustment response they have following placement of foster and adoptive children, benefits all family members.

10 These strategies have not been researched by any statistical, controlled study. However, anecdotal reports by foster and adoptive parents and caseworkers working on treatment teams underscore the general impactfulness of inventive strategies with certain disturbed children.

To order this book, please write to:

Horsetooth Press
P.O. Box 271036
Fort Collins, Colorado 80527

or contact the authors:

Dr. Frank R. Kunstal,   Phone: 970-223-9776   FAX 970-669-2157
Dr. Richard J. Delaney, Phone: 970-223-9669   FAX 406-683-9444

INDEX